Fire of Delay

Jill Robson

TRILOGY
PROFESSIONAL PUBLISHING MEETS POWERFUL PROMOTION
A wholly owned subsidiary of TBN

Fire of Delay

Trilogy Christian Publishers A Wholly Owned Subsidiary of Trinity Broadcasting Network

2442 Michelle Drive Tustin, CA 92780

Copyright © 2022 by Jill Robson

Rights Department, 2442 Michelle Drive, Tustin, CA 92780.

Trilogy Christian Publishing/TBN and colophon are trademarks of Trinity Broadcasting Network.

Cover design by: Christian Wenzel

For information about special discounts for bulk purchases, please contact Trilogy Christian Publishing.

Trilogy Disclaimer: The views and content expressed in this book are those of the author and may not necessarily reflect the views and doctrine of Trilogy Christian Publishing or the Trinity Broadcasting Network.

Manufactured in the United States of America

10 9 8 7 6 5 4 3 2 1

Library of Congress Cataloging-in-Publication Data is available.

ISBN: 979-8-88738-073-5

E-ISBN: 979-8-88738-074-2

This book is affectionately dedicated to my siblings, Tom, Sally, and Ally, who have journeyed through this fire with me, and to my beloved parents, who have now passed on to glory.

Acknowledgments

Writing this book has been one of the most rewarding and cathartic ventures I have undergone. None of it would have been possible without the investment and seeds that have been sown into my life by these incredible people in my life:

I am so grateful for my siblings, Sally, Tom, and Allyson, and how you help mold my life in Christ. Sally and Chuck, your marriage and the grace in which you received each other as a gift from God will forever be held up as an inspiration for what is to come for me. Sally, you may be my twin sister, but you are also my closest confidant, friend, and inspiration.

Tom and Hanna, you display the depth of friendship in marriage that I long for. The love and gratefulness I feel for you and the family can barely be expressed in words.

Ally, your journey of overcoming has inspired me so much, and you have always made me feel like a winner! So too have Jessica, Hailey, and Noah. I love you all.

Mom and Dad, you may not be here on this earth anymore, but I know you are surrounding me as part of the cloud of witnesses. Your encouragement for me to fly high and to be all God created me to be has been fuel for this journey more than anything else.

Ed and Ruth Silvoso, you have received me full-heartedly as family, and I love and honor you so much. Your marriage, your family, and all that you give away to this world have set me up to know that this fire of delay is fire unto glory!

Evelyn Silvoso Wallace, you are the most selfless boss, but most of all, you have become one of my closest friends and one of the most influential people in my life, and I am truly grateful for you.

Brian and Margaret Burton, this journey started with you in Phuket, Thailand! Without you, I am not sure where I would be today, and the fruit of your impartation to my life is seen in the entire family and me.

Laura Duncan, thank you for your insight into the compassion part and its power to break the yoke of shame.

Asaya Azah, my writing coach and editor, thank you for finally getting me to write this book. You have a true coaching gift.

Christian Wetzel, who always creates the most divinely inspired graphics. This cover is a testament to your gift!

Erika Faye Gottfredson, you are a true wordsmith and have helped me with the finishing touches.

Salome Roat, Become the One has been one of the most influential communities for me in San Jose, and I am very grateful for your friendship and inspiration.

Katie Harrison, my comrade on this journey of waiting for God's best. I am so blessed to have you as my dearest cousin and greatest champion for all that God has for us in our future kingdom marriages.

Caroline Oda, Gail Okuley, and Christina Battisti, I cannot thank you enough for your invaluable input as you reviewed the book and gave me inspiring feedback. Your work of love truly blessed me.

Finally, to my dearest friends who have been a part of getting this book completed over this last year: Helen Sinkinson, Susie Molina,

ACKNOWLEDGMENTS

Christine Starr, Heidi Joseph, Angelika Langner, Claudia Paterson, Emily Radonich, and Eli Brill. Thank you for your friendship, support, and love.

A Message from the Author

Much of what you will read in the following chapters is the revelation that I have received and the tools the Holy Spirit has given me to learn how to thrive in a season that seems like it will never end, all the while maintaining the expectancy that the Lord will bring victory at just the right time. My hope is that this book will give you the strength and encouragement to continue waiting and trusting in the Lord to fulfill His promises for you whilst seeing the transforming fire of His passionate love for you grow and manifest greater freedom in your soul.

Contents

Foreword

More than any time in history, we find ourselves in a culture that craves and expects instant gratification. Having to wait for anything is rarely seen as a positive experience, whether it be the minor inconvenience of a red traffic light or a delayed order at a drive-thru restaurant or the terrible grief experienced while awaiting a much-desired child after years of infertility treatments.

Today, cell phones allow us to make immediate connections. If the person at the other end of the line doesn't answer, we can text them. Gone are the days of landlines when we left a message on an answering machine and waited a day or two for a return call.

Microwaves provide instant meals; with Google, we find instant answers; using Amazon Prime, our purchases can be delivered the next day, sometimes even the same day. We just don't want to wait... for anything.

But what about the more life-altering things we often find ourselves waiting for? A spouse, a child, a career promotion, physical healing, financial provision? These are more than minor inconveniences, and we often struggle during the waiting, wondering if perhaps God has forgotten or overlooked us.

In *Fire of Delay*, Jill Robson has done a masterful job pouring out her own life experience, as she has walked closely with God through times of waiting. As spiritual parents to Jill, we have joined her on this walk on many occasions. It has not been easy. It has not been without pain and perplexity at times.

After dealing with the problem of pain and shame that leads to double-mindedness in section one of the book, in section two, she shares powerful perspectives she has received from God and His Word that have allowed her to keep her heart soft and intimate with Him. As a result, there has been a building of character, purity, trust, and vulnerability, which in addition to being a firm foundation for those things she is waiting for, has allowed her to minister to others who are walking a similar journey.

Finally, Jill provides practical tools in section three that will help you to minister to your soul and maintain a single mind while navigating delays in your life. *Strengthening yourself in the Lord* and *developing a grateful heart* are two such tools that will take you from a place of discouragement and hopelessness to great hope and expectation as you come into alignment with God's purpose and perspective for the area(s) where you may be facing delay.

We encourage you to begin this journey with an open heart and dependency on the Holy Spirit. Take advantage of the reflection questions at the end of each chapter and allow Him to speak to you. *"May the God of hope fill you with all joy and peace as you trust in him so that you will overflow with hope by the power of the Holy Spirit"* (Romans 15:13, NIV).

—Ed and Ruth Silvoso
Founders, Transform Our World

Introduction

My waiting journey began shortly after I had graduated as a sports therapist. I moved to Thailand and experienced a season of great favor work-wise. Simultaneously, I had just come out of a serious six-year relationship with a man I nearly married back in the UK. During this time in Phuket, God led me to Phuket Christian Center, where I was introduced to the Holy Spirit. This encounter transformed my very compromised walk with the Lord to a powerful journey of intimacy and surrender to Jesus. It was truly a precious time as I connected to other believers and allowed Jesus to do what my best friend called "open-heart surgery." During this time, I grew quickly in the Lord, as every part of my heart was exposed before Him to touch, to heal, to bring life to. It was like I finally was awakened to how the Lord saw and designed me. As a result, I was freed from an incredible amount of worldly junk, attitudes, and desires.

One of the noticeable changes I saw in myself had to do with my relationship with men. After being baptized in the Holy Spirit, I saw men differently.

An inner respect and honor started to grow, and I no longer needed men to meet my needs, emotionally or attention-wise. The way I knew God had done this work was that, for the first time in my life, I started to have married friends; women now trusted me around their husbands. This was a big deal, as it confirmed my change.

It was also during this time that I decided to seek the Lord's guidance for finding a husband. Having seen how my previous relationships had led to heartache, it seemed easy to ask Him for help in this area of my life. I took this very seriously and presented it to the Lord as an offering before Him, trusting His heart that if marriage was in the picture for me, He would affirm it in a tangible way over the coming weeks. And if not, He would show me and direct my path as to how to move forward. Either way, I knew I would be okay. I just wanted my life to be in His hands.

A week later, from a source I had not expected, God gave me His confirmation that His plan for my life did include marriage. An American gentleman, who had come to Phuket to marry his American fiancé, was the unexpected source. With her being a friend, I naturally jumped into helping pull off this last-minute wedding. It was wonderful! At the end of the reception, just after guests had waved off the newlyweds, this gentleman came back to where some of us were packing up. Walking up to me, he explained that he had been given a word by God for me earlier that morning and could not rest with his new bride until he shared it. He said, "Jill, the Lord showed me your heart, and you are His holy one, and God has someone He is preparing for you. Would you commit, in your heart, to wait for that man, whether it is five weeks, five months, five years, or longer? The Lord would not let me rest until I shared this message with you."

His demeanor was intense, as if he had carried this all day and needed to release it with integrity and sincerity. I acknowledged I had heard and received his message. Once I received it, he blessed me and left. I never saw him again.

It was overwhelmingly lovely to have the Holy Spirit minister so supernaturally in this way, and it settled my heart in knowing my desire for marriage was of Him and He would lead me to my husband. From that day on, I committed to honor my husband and wait with a sense of active expectancy by preparing myself in spirit, soul, and body. I became even more intentional about how I treated men and how I took care of myself. Life in this area shifted into a very secure space within my heart for many years.

Fast forward to 2010, when my internal battle began. I had just returned to the UK after fourteen years in Thailand and was staying with my parents in a sleepy town on the coast of England while I looked into what I would do next with my life. My twin sister was engaged; my best friend had just gotten married; my father was suffering with third-stage cancer, and although I knew I was led back to the UK, I could not find any job that fit my skills and passions. So I was feeling in a place of limbo despite my strong conviction to be there. Comparison, shame, and condemnation crept in my heart and dominated my thoughts and emotions.

I felt insecure and unsure of the future God had promised me, particularly concerning marriage. I was in unfamiliar territory; hope was low, and life seemed unbearably difficult.

Having never struggled with sleep issues, during this period, I would be awakened at night and tormented by the turmoil of my reality, my emotions, and the questions that swirled in my head and heart. The torment was real; the mocking voices were strong, and the internal pressure it produced kept me from sleeping night after night. I dreaded going to sleep, knowing what the night would entail. I would try to pray, focus on something else more life-giving or listen to music, but there was a draw within me that wanted to understand what was going on, find a solution, and fix it. I spent many of these nights processing with the Lord; however, I always ended up frustrated, offended, and angry. Here I was in the prime of life, pure, passionate, dedicated to the heart of God for my life, and yet, I was living in a place of lack and watching everyone around me walk out their dreams while my life seemed to be in a holding pattern. In Thailand, I learned to walk in the favor of the Lord and had always seen His hand on my life, but not now. It felt like I was being punished, and His hand had been removed. Nothing made sense.

After many weeks of sleepless nights and constantly trying to protect myself from my own thoughts and emotions, I had reached the point of pure exhaustion. Then one night, while soaking in the bathtub, I began to contemplate on how those around me saw my life, especially in comparison to my twin. And suddenly, I could feel their pity, and a picture of shame came upon me. It was heavy, and I felt crushed by the weight of this projected reality. In the middle of this pain, shame, and torment, I heard these quiet but powerful words within, "Jill, it is not others who are feeling sorry for you. It is you who is feeling sorry for you!" It was at this moment that everything changed. This simple statement shifted my perspective, helping me to see the pride I held in my own heart. I ignorantly did not realize I was leaning on my own understanding and my own interpretation of my life and had judged myself from a position that did not come from God. Like the final piece to a puzzle, I understood why I had lost my peace and, quite frankly, why I was no longer seeing favor in my life. That night, I decided to humble myself before God and completely let go of my understanding on the situation. Immediately, the fog lifted; the shame and guilt left, and, for the first time in a long time, I slept deeply and soundly.

Did the battles stop? No, they did not. However, the anchor of truth was now firmly placed within me to learn how to live a lifestyle of overcoming during seasons of extended waiting.

The Problem

Chapter 1

The Problem of Pain

"God whispers to us in our pleasures, speaks to us in our conscience, but shouts to us in our pain: it is His megaphone to rouse the deaf world."

—C. S. Lewis

The Problem of Pain

One of the hardest things I have faced over these last ten years is the inner battle that I have to regularly fight to live at peace in my heart regarding the unfulfilled promises of God. Though I have learned to live from a place of faith as a believer, a place where I can access the grace of God, I still find myself having to battle negative thinking, powerful emotions, and deep pain that has come from facing my physical reality. The unexpected turns of daily life and a strong sense of lack caused by entertaining lies have often left me feeling more like a failure than an overcomer.

It is like there are two Jills. One Jill, my true self, is kind, sweet, youthful, alive, and full of faith and intimacy with the Lord. This version of me rarely has difficulty believing all that God says is true. She gets excited about the smallest things, enjoys the moment, and thrives in relationships and connection with others. As this Jill, I know how to love others well, and I deeply desire to see people walk in the fullness of what Jesus paid for. I believe all things are possible, and I know I can go boldly before His throne of grace and receive His mercy and grace as needed. I naturally flow in the prophetic and always see the good in others. It is very rare for me to get offended by other people.

And then there is what I call "triggered Jill."

I say triggered, as it is not like I am two different people, and I certainly do not promote dualism of the good Jill versus the bad Jill, but like all of us, I get triggered by pain, by shame, and this inner dialogue that only ever leads to dark places. I have noticed over the years what can spark it and have worked to renew my mind in those areas, but I still find myself triggered by the reality of my life when I look at it from the perspective of the problem of not having a husband. Rarely does Jesus feel close to me when this happens, and in those brief times when He does, the illusion of separation is still there like a heavy blanket that clouds my thinking, my emotions, and my processing. Shame is nearly always present, and so is condemnation.

The torment on these occasions pulls my heart into a place of unbelief and sadness. I know torment, shame, and condemnation never come from the Lord, and so I have done my best to deal with them spiritually by using the power of the Word, tongues, worship, and standing in my authority as God's beloved child. In Christ, there is only one enemy, the devil. However, much of my journey has been a battle within my soul. Even so, bit by bit, the love of God has opened my eyes to His compassion, where I am convinced it is possible to come to a place where you never have to have a bad day! I know it is a pretty radical statement, and you might be thinking, *She has truly lost her mind!* But before you cast your judgment and label me as crazy, let me explain what I mean a bit further.

As so many scriptures have reminded us, there is a fierce battle happening in the spirit realm: God's angels versus the fallen ones. However, I believe there is an even greater battle that does not often get talked about, and that is the battle within our soul and how our experience with it shapes the way we see things and what we choose to believe about ourselves. It is at the place of the soul where the temptation to judge our lives from an earthly perspective rather than a heavenly perspective is battled. The question we must ask ourselves is: Will we choose to settle for facts, or will we choose to believe the truth of God's promises?

This book is an inside view into navigating the journey of the soul to a place of revelation, peace, and dominion. The best way to describe this journey would be like viewing a landscape from a plane flying in the air rather than from a location on the ground. When we gain this perspective, the freedom in the soul is explosive because the truth that sets us free is now our reality and no longer just a longing of the heart.

Gaining God's perspective on what is really going on in my life has helped me navigate this season of extended delay and has taught me how to thrive knowing the joy set before me.

While singleness has been the focus of delay for me, what about you? What is on your heart that you have been waiting for? What desire or dream has God deposited in your heart and promised to fulfill that is still dormant? Is it a career? A child? A desire to see a family member or friend saved? We all have different things that can fit this question; however, the struggle is still the same.

Chapter 2

The Problem of Shame

"And the man and his wife were both naked,
but they were not ashamed."

Genesis 2:25 (NASB)

Pain Caused by Shame

I am convinced that the most debilitating form of pain is shame and its impact on our very sense of identity. It is something I became very familiar with as I walked faithfully with the Lord, observing others living and walking into marriage and starting families, from my generation to the next, and feeling this sense that it was out of reach for me. Now, that is not true, and anyone who knows me will agree, but what I have noticed is when a person is in emotional pain and in deep need, receiving truth with no compassion attached to it will often feel more like condemnation.

As a result, rather than feeling encouraged, that person is left feeling shame.

So what is shame exactly? Shame is any area of your life where you do not feel like you are enough, seen, heard, or accepted. We often recognize shame as a response to doing something bad, but that is actually guilt. Shame is much deeper and much more connected to who we are rather than what we have done. Brene Brown, in her book *Daring Greatly*, explains guilt as, "I did something bad," while shame is, "I am bad."

When we take a look at what happened to Adam and Eve after they ate the forbidden fruit, we see they experienced shame and not guilt. Genesis 3:7 (NLT) states, *"At that moment their eyes were opened, and they [Adam and Eve] suddenly felt shame at their nakedness. So they sewed fig leaves together and made coverings for themselves."* Before they ate from the Tree of Knowledge, they were "naked and knew no shame" (Genesis 2:25). Shame, not guilt, was the first response when man disobeyed God. Consequently, a new identity was created for humanity—one based on shame and hiding.

As demonstrated by Adam and Eve, shame leads to hiding. For them, it was literal, but, for us, our hiding occurs in the soul realm and is more psychological.

Today, psychology is showing some incredible insights into this. We have what psychologists call hard, big emotions like anger, fear, rejection, and despair that we hide behind to protect ourselves.

> We often don't realize we are doing it, but we hide behind these hard, weighty, very powerful emotions to protect the softer, tender, vulnerable emotions connected to shame.

These emotions need to be met with compassion and comfort for healing from shame to start to take place. What I have noticed from experience, however, is that we rarely get to these more vulnerable emotions because we get stuck in the cycle of shame.

This cycle starts with hiding. Negative experiences and trauma, especially as children, can lead to deep shame that can remain unresolved into adulthood. In order to protect ourselves, we then hide behind those powerful, harder emotions like fear and anger. Yet, the issue is these types of emotions are designed for protection and cannot easily be ministered to, or they mask what is really going on underneath.

What we really want is to deal with the deeper, softer, and tender emotions. However, when the softer emotions arise, they can be overlooked because the harder emotions of fear, rejection, anger, and despair are so consuming that we think these are the ones we need to deal with. We can spend so much time living consumed by these emotions that what is really going on gets overlooked and never fully gets ministered to.

This is where the cycle gets perpetuated.

When we get triggered, shame rises up, and along with it, the harder, protective emotions. Since we, ultimately, need comfort, we subconsciously find ourselves running to familiar, immediate comforts like spiritual activity, food, and TV binging. On the extreme end, drugs, unhealthy relationships, alcoholism, and other addictions can become our comforts. A calm always takes place when comfort is administered, even if it is unhealthy. Yet, because the root issue of shame has not been dealt with, we are left vulnerable to experience the cycle once more until it is finally addressed.

One day, I remember I called my twin. I was so angry at God and shouting at the top of my voice from the pain I was in. I had what looked like a ridiculous fight with a hanger, getting caught behind another in my closet, and, to make things worse, one of my pockets got stuck on the door at the same time. It triggered something in me completely unconnected to the poor hanger. Unbeknownst to me, the cycle of shame was at work.

Rather than taking everything at face value, Sally just listened to me. As she listened and got me breathing, she gently acknowledged my emotions by saying things like, "That must really hurt" or "What's your heart really feeling?" "I hear you" to get past those hard emotions. That is when I realized that my anger was in the fact that I felt forgotten, unseen, and left out of God's personal blessings. It was then that Sally could minister to me by addressing that my core issue was that I felt like I had no value to God. This was the root issue at play in this situation. After I calmed down, I was able to move on with my day.

An important note to make is the physiological impact on the body when we go through this shame cycle. Those hard, big emotions I previously mentioned, like fear, anger, and rejection, are the emotions that take us into what we call "fight or flight." The back part of our brain, which is wired to help us escape from a predator like an oncoming car or wild animal, is activated, releasing adrenaline into the body. Our heart rate increases, and the rest of the body goes into shut-down mode, sending oxygen to the legs, arms, and skin, so the focus can be on running away from the predator. If this mechanism is not switched off and brought back into equilibrium, the muscles, joints, thyroid, skin, and intestines can be negatively affected. Panic attacks become frequent, even in our sleep. All of this turmoil is due to unaddressed shame.

The Origin of Shame

As I have let the Lord lead me to understand more about shame and what really happened in the garden with Adam and Eve, more and more, I have come to realize that shame is at the root of nearly every issue, every disease, and sickness, and it is something every believer has to deal with on some level or another.

Why? Because until Adam and Eve had their eyes opened to the knowledge of good and evil, they knew no shame. They were naked before they ate the fruit and lived in total harmony with God and their surroundings. Yet, somehow, after eating that fruit, their eyes were opened to a vulnerability and weakness they had never experienced before. In the blink of an eye, being naked in front of one another and God was now shameful.

Shame led them to cover themselves, and when they heard God, instead of meeting Him as they usually did in the cool of the day, they were afraid and hid from Him. Why is this important? Because the Tree of Knowledge of Good and Evil is the knowledge of both evil and good! Not just evil.

Both the evil and the good lead to shame! It is not that anything good is actually evil because, as we know, one of the fruits of the Spirit in Galatians 6 is goodness. My aim here is to show that good and evil are on the same spectrum of how we process and judge our circumstances as one or the other.

However, we were originally designed to filter our circumstances through the perspective of life, where every thought is yielded to Christ. Since we are the offspring of Adam and Eve, our eyes are now open to our nakedness, which is also our weakness and our vulnerability—our inability apart from God. As a result, it has become natural to hide ourselves from others and especially from Him because of shame.

There were two trees in the garden of Eden, and God's original intent was for us to eat from the Tree of Life, but things drastically changed the day Adam and Eve sinned against God. Consequently, it has led many of us to eat from the wrong tree. However, there is good news! Through the cross, Jesus has given us a pathway back to live according to God's original design for us and eat from the Tree of Life again.

You Know a Tree by Its Fruit

One of the signs that we are feeding from the Tree of Knowledge of Good and Evil is a sense of separation from God. It is an illusion, but it is still an awareness that leads to shame. Shame causes us to hide and prevents the true need of our heart—the Lord's compassion—from being met. Shame is a response to both the knowledge and the awareness of good and evil. We can easily understand that acts and thoughts of evil defile us and create a sense of humiliation, but what about good? In my opinion, it is almost worse than evil. How so? Let me give you an example. The shame I have carried in my heart, which really manifested itself as a response to being single, childless, and unsettled, caused me to subtly try to be "good" before God. I did my best to live a Holy Spirit–filled life, but, as we now know, this was just a cover to what the real issue was.

Shame, like I said before, comes with big emotions that put us into fight or flight mode. For me, subtle bursts of anger against God and myself would manifest. No matter how much ministry I received, I could not get to the bottom of where this anger was coming from. Ultimately, I realized that what I was experiencing were symptoms of a deeper issue of shame that I had not yet addressed.

Adam and Eve hid, but God never separated Himself from them. He still walked in the garden to meet them, looking for connection. His questions to them were ones to draw them out of hiding, not to add to their shame: *"But the LORD God called to Adam, and said to him, 'Where are you?' 'Who told you that you were naked?'"* (Genesis 3:9, 11, AMP). In other words, "Who said you were not enough? Who said you were unworthy, bad, and had no value?" Interesting that here we see God's compassion even with His first question to Adam and Eve. Now, look at Adam's response to God, *"...the woman You gave me..."* (Genesis 3:12, NLT). Rather than acknowledging the shame that he was feeling and allowing himself to receive God's healing compassion, Adam goes into fight mode with his feelings of anger and accusation toward God.

Compassion is something every human being needs because all mankind is exposed to the knowledge of good and evil. Although we are believers, we can still fall back into living from this place of knowledge, even once we have "returned" to the Tree of Life. We must remember, in those moments of shame, that God has never separated Himself from us. Therefore, His compassion is extended toward us. All we have to do is receive it.

I understand that receiving God's compassion for us is not always easy. In the strategies section of this book, I will address some practical ways for you to implement to help you receive and minister compassion to yourself in this season of extended delay.

Reflection Questions

When you think of the word "shame," what comes to mind and what emotions rise up in you?

_____

_____

_____

_____

_____

What are some memories that come to mind when you contemplate on the subject of shame?

_____

_____

_____

_____

_____

THE PROBLEM OF SHAME

What areas of your life do you want to keep hidden? Can you articulate why?

_____

_____

_____

_____

_____

Chapter 3

Governing Your Soul

"...he that is lord of his soul, is better than an overcomer of cities."

Proverbs 16:32 (WYC)

Governing Your Soul

When we experience periods of extended delay and hardships that we know are contrary to God's promises, personal revelation, and prophetic words, we face powerful emotions and subtle thoughts that try to help us understand what is happening. The pressure in processing these emotions and thoughts is like an unrestrained tornado within our soul. Though we know of characters in the Bible who have overcome great things, we can find ourselves entertaining the lies that lead to hopelessness and depression.

Learning to navigate the waters of our soul is no small feat. As I meditated on this incredible proverb, "Greater is he who can control his own soul than he who can take a city," I realized that the soul is probably the hardest area to bring under the control of the Holy Spirit. There is not a believer on this earth who does not have to learn how to take his or her thoughts captive and control their emotions. As the proverb indicates, our greatest battle is not external to us but rather within us.

I find the idea of a city being easier to govern than one's own soul to be quite fascinating. More so because I work and minister with an incredible organization called Transform Our World (TOW), whose sole purpose is to transform cities and nations around the world. Over the years, TOW has become one of the world's leading organizations in this area of transformation. Even with as many challenges as TOW has faced in bringing transformation to cities and nations, it is still easier than bringing transformational change to one's soul. Wow!

Even so, the truth is God, our Father, has given us what I will call strategies and tools to navigate and overcome the realms of the soul and understand His kingdom as well as our design and how to overcome anything that gets thrown at us. Picture with me a pilot flying a Cessna in clear blue skies, enjoying the rush of adrenaline and beauty of the scenery below as he makes his way to his destination. He can see clearly; he only needs to look with his eyes whether to go up or down, pull back on the throttle a little or increase it.

Then, unexpectedly, a storm comes. Clouds descend on the once clear blue sky, and the pilot's reliance on his natural senses to direct him can no longer be trusted. Now, in the middle of a storm, he has lost his sense of direction. Remembering the stories of pilots who flew directly toward the ground believing they were flying straight, the pilot, not willing to take the risk, turns to the plane's navigation system for help. This allows him to put his trust in something greater than his natural senses to get him safely to his destination. Just as in life, some storms are unexpected. Learning how to use the right tools is key not only for our safety but our survival as well. The difference between life and death or joy and suffering when we are going through a difficult life season depends on what we decide to put our trust in.

It is during times of waiting on the promises of God that, like the pilot who could no longer just trust his natural senses, we, too, must rely on something greater than our own human understanding. Similar to the pilot's navigation system, there are tools and strategies that God has given us in His Word to overcome every storm we face, every wilderness we go through, and every weapon formed against us.

In addition to His Word, we have the greatest blessing on earth: His Holy Spirit dwelling inside of us. We are the temple of the Holy Spirit, and the Bible tells us in John 14 and John 16 that the Holy Spirit is our "advocate, counselor, and our comforter," and in 1 John, we are reminded that the Holy Spirit Himself will teach us.

Self-control or temperance, as some translations put it, is a fruit of the Holy Spirit, as discussed in Galatians 6:22. For the sake of uniformity, we will use the word self-governance instead of self-control. Ultimately, self-governance is the fruitful work of the Holy Spirit within us, which He is committed to cultivating in our lives.

The things I write and share here in this book are not methods or a set of laws to follow, but wisdom gleaned from revelation, experience, and intimacy with the living God. Very often, the way the Lord is leading those closest to you, your spouse, neighbor, best friend, or confidant, is different from the way He is guiding you. Acknowledging this and learning to honor that the Holy Spirit in you is able to guide you even in the midst of difficulty is important.

Can I pray for you?

Heavenly Father, I pray for each person reading this book that Your Holy Spirit would cultivate a sensitivity to the transforming work You are doing as they read the words on these pages. Your words are Spirit and life, and I pray that their eyes would be opened to who they truly are, that Your Spirit within them would become the governing force within their minds, healing their hearts and bringing the fullness of all You have for them into manifestation on earth. In Jesus' mighty name, amen.

So What Exactly Is the Soul?

The soul is a complicated thing carefully designed by God for the fulfillment of all He has for us on this earth and the mediator between the spirit and earthly realms.

We were created by God as a triune being: spirit, soul, and body. When God created man, He declared it "good," and it is important to keep this in the front of our mind when processing what can feel like very dark and negative emotions. Though there are numerous passages on the soul in both the Old Testament and the New Testament, we can see a pattern of the triune aspect of the believer in 1 Thessalonians 5:23 (NIV):

"May God, Himself, the God of peace, sanctify you through and through. May your whole spirit, soul and body be kept blameless at the coming of our Lord Jesus Christ."

The body is the physical part of us that we see in the mirror. The Greek word for "the physical body" is *soma*. It is different from the word that means "the flesh," which in Greek is *sarx*. *Sarx* refers to the carnal nature of things.

The soul, however, is not as tangible as the body.

In the scripture passage above, the word used for "soul" is "psyche," which we know is made up of the mind, will, emotions, imagination, and potentially, other parts of our being, such as our reasoning.

Because these influence the way we filter and experience the world and how we express these things outwardly, many would call this collective unit our personality.

We actually see in the Old Testament that different aspects of the soul are depicted as physical organs of the body, which further shows the incredible complexity of it. The heart, for example, is used metaphorically to mean the moral and emotionally-intellectual part of us. Very often, the heart and mind are used interchangeably throughout the Word to represent the soul but also the human spirit.

We Can Touch the Body and the Soul

Though the body can be touched physically, the soul, too, can be touched by words, which have the power to impact us emotionally and mentally. These two parts of who we are are constantly being touched! The words we hear from our environment growing up, culture, education, and friendships all "touch" the soul. Basically, our experiences speak to us all the time. Good or bad, they create thought processes within us, conscious and unconscious, that build up an atmosphere around us. It is important to note that emotions follow our thoughts. They are not mutually exclusive. In fact, emotions are the chemical responses created from within the brain, which come from thought processes. This is why the renewing of the mind is referred to in the Bible rather than the processing of emotions, which are the result of the thought process itself.

I find it interesting that, during the hardest times, it is emotional pain due to fear, rejection, or abandonment that tends to scream the loudest at us rather than what we are thinking. We can find ourselves responding from emotion to emotion and yet, never actually getting to the root of what is really going on in the mind. We will unwrap this more at different points as we go along, but what is important to remember here is the impact words have on the human soul.

Let us take a look at the final and most incredible part of us, our spirit. In John 3:6 (NASB), Jesus says, *"That which is born of the spirit is spirit and that which is born of the flesh is flesh."* The spirit cannot be accessed physically. The spirit part of us is where God communicates directly with us because God is Spirit (John 4:24). It helps us to remember that God is not a mind; He is Spirit. We are not just awakened to the things of God when we are born again, but we literally become a new creation! A new species.

It is in our spirit that this transformation occurs. Nowhere else.

"Therefore, if anyone is in Christ, the new creation has come. The old has gone, the new is here!" (2 Corinthians 5:17, NIV)

Our spirit is made perfect, justified by the Lord, and sanctified already through our belief in Jesus. Our conscience, which is a faculty of our spirit, is cleansed by His blood.

> *Therefore, brethren, since we have confidence to enter the holy place by the blood of Jesus, by a new and living way which He inaugurated for us through the veil, that is, His flesh, and since we have a great priest over the house of God, let us draw near with a sincere heart in full assurance of faith, having our hearts sprinkled clean from an evil conscience and our bodies washed with pure water.*
>
> Hebrews 10:19–22 (NASB)

It is the soul part of us that needs to come into alignment with our spirit in order for us to truly believe God and receive the goodness He has made available to us through His Son, Jesus Christ. The only way this can happen is through the transformational experience of sanctifying our souls. Very much like the way a baby matures to a child and then to an adult, so too does a Christ-redeemed soul grow. As you can see, this is not an overnight process. It requires time, patience, and humility.

Thankfully, God is patient, and the Holy Spirit is willing to help us learn how to walk in the freedom Jesus has given to us.

Even with the Holy Spirit's help, the battle to govern our soul is the hardest battle we will ever have to face. Why?

Because the very nature of the soul will commonly accept facts as evidence.

On its own, the soul has no ability to process information outside of the physical realm. However, for us believers, this is completely contrary to the truth of God's Word, where we are called to live by faith and not by sight.

The struggle between living by "physical evidence" versus living by "evidence not yet seen" could not be more apparent than during times when we face delay. When the facts of our reality have not yet produced the physical answer to our prayers, we can come to a place where we pronounce judgment on God and His love for us as a lie. In these moments, the voice of the lie speaks louder than the truth of who God and His love for us is.

I remember when I first encountered the incredible baptism of the Holy Spirit in my early twenties. Having not known anything about this dimension of salvation, I was immediately delivered from a history of self-hate that had manifested itself in having anorexic tendencies throughout my teen years. Since this spiritual encounter with the Holy Spirit, I have not struggled in this area again. Yet, there have been many areas where my mind has needed to be renewed and my heart healed. The process of doing so has taken years, not days. My journey to mind-renewal and heart-healing has been very much like a rollercoaster ride. In the spirit, I accepted the truth of God's Word that the areas I was struggling with had been taken care of. However, my mind could not process this acceptance, and my emotions ran wild. The reality of my current situation was stronger than the faith to know things had changed and an inner battle would wage within me. This, my friend, is what we are dealing with when it comes to the pain of delayed answers to prayer.

> While we are seeking after answered prayers, God is seeking after our hearts, and, in the process, He brings His perspective, revealing to us the mind of Christ, which not only transforms us but gives the ability for our spirit to reign over our soul.

This then allows us to permanently live in a belief atmosphere where all things are possible with God.

But remember, this is a journey!

Earlier, I mentioned I work and minister at Transform Our World, and I can honestly say that some of the most powerful teachings I have ever heard on the transformation of the soul have come from its founder, Dr. Ed Silvoso. Please know that I do not make this endorsement lightly. I have read a lot of material and have listened to countless hours of teachings from wonderful teachers over the past couple of decades, and he is one of the best teachers, if not the best, on the subject of strongholds and the battle in the heavenly realms. I encourage you, if you have not already read his material, to check out his books *That None Should Perish* and *Prayer Evangelism* and the booklet *Strongholds*.

Ed and his wife, Ruth, are to be honored for the paths they have paved in the transformation of nations, and in his books, you see the significance of transformation taking place not only in cities and nations but within individual people, marriages, and families as well as within our spheres of influence.

Transformation is not about one area of life over another. It is about all areas of life changing under God's glory and power. As God has shown me how to govern my soul, the focus on the transformation of my family, city, and nation has become clearer.

Reflection Questions

Can you recognize the difference between your spirit and your soul? Write down how you recognize the difference.

_____

_____

_____

_____

_____

Can you see how what you are thinking affects your emotions? Write a couple of examples where what you were thinking affected your emotions in a good way.

_____

_____

_____

_____

_____

Can you trace back any negative emotions you have experienced to negative thinking?

_____

_____

_____

_____

_____

Can you see how our experiences in life can speak to us, both good and bad?

_____

_____

_____

_____

_____

If you answered yes to the previous question, can you see the impact of this on the soul, which accepts facts as evidence rather than the truth of the Word of God?

_____

_____

_____

_____

_____

Chapter 4

The Soul Needs a Spiritual Habitation

So then ye are no more strangers and sojourners, but ye are fellow-citizens with the saints, and of the household of God, being built upon the foundation of the apostles and prophets, Christ Jesus, Himself, being the chief cornerstone; in whom each several building, fitly framed together, groweth into a holy temple in the Lord; in whom ye also are builded together for a habitation of God in the Spirit.

Ephesians 2:19–22 (ASV)

The Mold of the Soul

One of the things I have found interesting over the years is understanding how the soul was created to live in a spiritual habitation.

Originally, when man was created in the garden of Eden, the soul was in God. It lived in the realm of light. Adam's will was yielded to God, and he was one with God. He was made in God's image, created to reign in the garden and to bring the dominion of the garden to the outermost places of the earth.

When Adam and Eve had to leave the garden, their soul needed a dwelling place because the atmosphere of the garden was lost due to sin entering in. They, thus, entered the dwelling place of darkness. We could also describe this as the realm of the devil and confusion. Many call this the "fallen" state, which is lower and less than the original design of God.

Interestingly, this, too, is built around sound and frequency.

Voices and words that we hear are sounds and frequencies that affect the formation of the soul. As Ana Mendez puts it, the soul is like a mold that is formed by the voices (words and sounds) we hear. Molds are formations of pliable material that can change shape given their environment.

> This is incredibly significant because words, therefore, affect our soul and its health. They literally create the habitation that impacts and shapes the soul.

When God created man, He created him in the perfect spiritual habitation, the garden of Eden. It was here where our souls were molded by the voice of truth through perfect communion with God Himself. The wholeness of our being was in full expression of life, truth, and absolute oneness with the Spirit of God, where believing was not a problem.

After the fall, mankind was subjected to a new habitation, as it had to leave the garden. The frequencies (voices and sounds) of darkness caused the soul of man to think lower, to struggle with trusting and believing God, and to no longer be aligned with the power of the truth for which we were made.

Thankfully, through Jesus' death and resurrection, our soul has been restored back to its original habitation.

The words we hear speak to us; the experiences we go through speak to us; memories speak to us; the world around us speaks to us; culture speaks to us; education speaks to us; music speaks to us. We are hearing words all the time, and they are constantly framing up a habitation for our soul.

This revelation is incredibly powerful because this is where the mind comes in. What we meditate on, soak in, and saturate ourselves in impacts the spiritual atmosphere and, therefore, the health of our souls. So although growing up you may have been subjected to a negative environment, where words were used to hurt, defile, or bring harm, you have the ability within you to change the atmosphere. Through this change, you then can create the perfect spiritual habitation for your soul to experience oneness with the Spirit of God.

Dr. Caroline Leaf has spent much of her life's research changing what used to be believed about how our thought life impacts the brain. What is quite fascinating is that her research confirms Romans 12:1–2, where Paul exhorts us to be transformed by the renewing of our minds. She has shown that our brain wiring can actually be changed by the process called neuroplasty.

She says:

> *Thoughts are real, physical things that occupy mental real estate. Moment by moment, every day, you are changing the structure of your brain through your thinking. When we hope, it is an activity of the mind that changes the structure of our brain in a positive and normal direction.*

Now, let us take this a step further.

You Are in the Word

Extended delay has a way of bringing up everything that may have been hidden in our hearts that needs to be healed, overcome, or touched by God's love. When there is wounding in our hearts and our minds have not been renewed, it can become difficult to believe the truth of God's Word, a truth that truly sets us free.

Before we proceed any further, I would like you to spend some time reading and saturating yourself in the following passages. As you are doing so, allow yourself to become aware of the atmosphere around you and His presence.

John 15:5 (NIV):

"I am the vine; you are the branches. If you remain in Me and I in you, you will bear much fruit; apart from Me you can do nothing."

Psalm 62:1 (NIV):

"Truly my soul finds rest in God; my salvation comes from Him."

Romans 8:1 (NIV):

"Therefore there is now no condemnation at all for those who are in Christ Jesus."

Galatians 3:26 (NIV):

"So in Christ Jesus you are all children of God through faith."

Ephesians 2:6 (NIV):

"And God raised us up with Him, and seated us with Him in the heavenly places in Christ Jesus."

Romans 8:9 (NASB):

"You, however, are not in the flesh but in the Spirit, if in fact the Spirit of God dwells in you."

Ephesians 4:24 (NIV):

"And to put on the new self, created after the likeness of God in true righteousness and holiness."

Although the Word can speak to us as we read it, we are also "in" the Word because Jesus Himself is the Word who was made flesh (John 1:1–3). As the previous passages suggest, throughout the New Testament, we see the phrase "in" Him used many times. Being "in

Him" is the habitation we were originally designed for and is the habituation we must return to.

Since receiving this understanding, I have done my best to saturate myself "in" Him, in His presence, as well as in reading His Word. As a result, I have become more aware of the atmosphere around me and how my soul is responding to it. If at any point I start to have feelings of condemnation, disappointment, or hopelessness, I begin to speak into the atmosphere, declaring the Word of God as though I am cocooning myself in the spiritual atmosphere of His presence.

As I declare His words of truth and life, I feel my countenance change; my spirit emerges, and my soul takes a back seat.

God's spiritual atmosphere is accessible to all of us twenty-four seven. We do not have to travel far to get to it.

However, it does take practice to be able to cultivate this spiritual atmosphere.

Learning to Minister to Your Soul

In this book, my desire is to get across that you and I, as believers, have been given something special: the Holy Spirit. He is our great "Comforter" and "Counselor." His living presence within us has made it possible to live a life where we do not just turn to others for help, but by His direction, we learn how to minister to ourselves. I like to call this our "Holy Spirit empowerment."

We read in the Old Testament that the prophets longed to see the day when God would abide "in" men, and we are living it (Matthew 13:17). It is easy to take this for granted, but the more I have allowed myself to be yielded to the guidance of the wonderful Holy Spirit, the more I have seen how powerful His ministry is to me and how He directs me to live in a place of belief where I can receive all that Jesus has paid for on the cross.

In the New Testament, there are three passages, Hebrews 3:13, Ephesians 5:18, and Colossians 3:16, that talk about ministering to our souls. Unfortunately, most translations have translated these passages incorrectly. And as a result, the truth and power that come with these passages have not been fully received by many in the body of Christ. In Hebrews 3:13, Ephesians 5:18, and Colossians 3:16, there is a Greek word, *heautou*, that many have translated to mean "one another" as in the context of ministering to one another. Look them up in your Bible. You will see they say minister to "one another." However, the Greek word for "one another" is *alilis* and not *heautou*. The true meaning of *heautou* is "yourself." So, by definition, all three scriptures are essentially saying, "Minister to yourself! Exhort yourself!"

Let us take a look at these three passages using the correct translation:

Hebrews 3:13 (NIV):

"But encourage [yourself] daily, as long as it is called 'Today,' so that none of you may be hardened by sin's deceitfulness."

Ephesians 5:18–20 (NASB):

And do not get drunk with wine, for that is dissipation, but be filled with the Spirit, speaking to yourselves in psalms and hymns and spiritual songs, singing and making melody with your heart to the Lord; always giving thanks for all things in the name of our Lord Jesus Christ to God, even the Father.

Colossians 3:16 (NASB):

"Let the word of Christ richly dwell within you, with all wisdom teaching and admonishing yourself with psalms and hymns and spiritual songs, singing with thankfulness in your hearts to God."

Just a simple change to the correct translation and the meaning and impact of the passage are completely different. How powerful it is to know that we can learn to minister to our soul! It further affirms the truth that we can take control of our soul and bring it into alignment with the Holy Spirit to manifest the true design for which we were created!

Even though it is good and important for us to minister to one another, it is just as important for us to know that we have access to a lifestyle of encouraging ourselves in His Word with songs, hymns, psalms, and thankfulness. Just look at King David, for example, who would minister and speak to his soul.

"Why art thou cast down, O my soul? And why art thou disquieted within me? Hope thou in God; for I shall yet praise him for the help of his countenance" (Psalm 42:5, KJV).

The Answer Is Within

Remember, when we are facing delay and what seems like unanswered prayers, it is very important for us to realize that the answer to navigating the emotional rollercoaster that waiting brings is within us. We do not have to look outside of ourselves for rescue. Under the leadership of the Holy Spirit, we have been given the power to renew our minds, pull down strongholds, and heal our broken hearts by ministering to our souls.

A Miraculous Lesson in the Power of Ministering to My Soul

In 2012, I was walking out this revelation and was learning how to thrive. I was in Phuket on a short vacation visiting church family, and I had to get my house in order after having a tenant who had not taken care of the property. The place was a mess, and it seemed like everything needed addressing, including the drains, which were all clogged. I did not have any drain cleaner, so I had to go to the local store to buy it. The typical product I usually got was not there; instead, the Thai gentleman advised me to use a product that I later discovered was one of the most dangerous products on the market. It was so dangerous even construction workers did not use it.

In my obvious ignorance, I went home and proceeded to pour the drain cleaner down the first drain. And, to my amazement, it cleared rather quickly. I was so impressed that I called my friend Helen, who was staying with me at the time, so she could see how well the drain cleaner was working. Just as I was getting ready to pour it down the next drain, by the grace of God, Helen suggested I not stand over the sink. I stepped back as I poured the acid down the drain.

The next few minutes are what I will describe to you as surreal. As the acid hit the blockage, the entire contents burst back out of the sink onto me and all the items around the sink. The acid was so strong that as it hit my stomach and my left leg, it immediately burned a hole through my clothes. My skin started to bubble, and in a period of just a few seconds, I screamed, ripped off my clothes, and ran out of the bathroom I was in and into the other bathroom to get water.

As I entered the second bathroom, a wave of shock hit me, and I could feel myself start to faint. I held onto the door, hoping I could collect myself. That is when I caught a glimpse of myself in the mirror. Like an automatic switch, something triggered inside of me, and I shifted out of this place of emotional panic, pain, and fear. I looked into my eyes, and I began to pray in the spirit. It was so quick, but all of a sudden, I started to calm down.

Still looking into the mirror, I stared into my eyes and began to thank God that I had stepped back and that the acid had not hit my face. I spoke peace and blessings to my body, to my skin, to my stomach and leg. I grabbed a wet towel and dabbed the area, attempting to remove the acid from my skin. Even though by this point blisters and blood were visible, I still spoke peace to the situation and instructed Helen to look up what to do with an acid burn. Clearly, this was not a sign of a person in panic or stress! Instead of allowing the fear to take over me, I resisted and focused intently on speaking peace and blessing over myself. All the while, I continued to dab the area of my stomach that was burned while Helen searched for the answer. This was all in the space of a few minutes.

She eventually found instructions that informed us that any acid burn bigger than a couple of inches required medical attention. By the looks of it, the burn was definitely more than a few inches. I quickly changed my clothes to wear something looser, and we jumped into the car to go to the hospital.

The entire ride, Helen and I just blessed my body, focused on Jesus, and prayed in tongues. As we drove, the story of the man who fell out the window and died because he fell asleep while listening to Paul preach came to my mind, and I shared it with Helen. We both started laughing because, in the same way, one would think, *Who falls asleep near an open window?* It was equally as silly to pour an acid that is banned in Europe, mind you, down a drain!

Although the story came to mind quite randomly, as we know, nothing is by coincidence with God.

Sensing there was a lesson the Holy Spirit was trying to reveal, we decided to pray into it. I began to thank God that the same power that was available to raise the man who fell from the window and died was also available to me. While we were praying, I had a wet towel on my stomach and another wet towel that I was dabbing on my left leg. Suddenly, when I looked down at my leg, I noticed that the blisters and the red, bloody area underneath them had almost disappeared. I thought to myself, *Hmmm, how strange!* If I can be fully transparent, even though we were praying for my healing, I was not expecting a miracle. So I asked Helen with slight confusion in my voice, "Can blisters just disappear?" Looking back, being that I was the one trained in healthcare, I think it is quite funny that I asked her this question. Of course, I knew this was not normal, but I believe I needed reassurance that I was, indeed, experiencing a supernatural miracle.

Curious, I lifted up my dress and looked under the towel that was on my belly, and I saw the same thing happening. The area that was blistered and, at one point, bubbling under the acid was now looking like skin that had never been burned. As I laid hands on myself and blessed my body, right in front of my eyes, the burned areas shrank.

By the time we got to the hospital, there was only a tiny area left on my stomach. I knew something amazing was happening, but just to be sure I was okay, we went into the hospital. When the doctor came in, I explained to him what had happened, but he could not believe that I had been burned by acid. Having had knowledge of the drain cleaner I used, he said it was not possible for my skin to look the way it did. The doctor said what I had was nothing more than a sunburn. A sunburn! Can you believe it!

I tried to re-explain to him what happened, but this time in Thai, and he just looked at me confused.

Looking at my vitals, he noted my blood pressure was completely normal and because my demeanor seemed to be excited-like, he thought either I was confused about what really happened to me, or I did not understand his Thai. Fair enough! It is not every day you have a patient who does not actually need to be a patient!

Still in awe, Helen and I drove back home, and later that night, as I lay in bed revisiting the day with the Lord and thanking Him, He spoke to my heart, "Jill, you saw My power manifest in an incredible way today, in an extreme situation, as you brought your soul into alignment with your spirit and My leading. But what about bringing this into the day-to-day experiences of life that you face that are not yet as you would like them, ministering to your soul by exhorting yourself in My truth and love? This same power will transform you as you allow your mind to be governed by the Holy Spirit, taking thoughts captive and encouraging yourself in Me, ministering the power of peace and blessing to your soul."

As I meditated on this, it helped shift me more into the awareness of developing a "lifestyle" of encouraging myself in the Lord and allowing the Holy Spirit to lead me internally. Romans 8:6 (NASB) reminds us of this fact, "*For the mind set on the flesh is death, but the mind set on the Spirit is life and peace.*"

It is important you know that power lies within you. The Holy Spirit is committed to leading you, counseling you, and guiding you just like Jesus told us He would in John 16.

Respectfully, we need to acknowledge that we are not victims of our circumstances and in need of constant outside help, but rather quite powerful in every moment, no matter what it looks like. Peace is the plumb line for you and me to measure and respond to, and the ways to minister to our soul are endless.

Do not fall for the lie that you are powerless when you face seasons of extended waiting. You will see in the final chapter that I unwrap some key tools for you to use to minister to your soul, which will help bring perspective as to how peace and stability can reign in your life.

Reflection Questions

What are some of the things you have learned to do to encourage yourself in the Lord during times of waiting and uncertainty?

_____

_____

_____

_____

_____

What did the testimony of the "acid burn miracle" reveal to you?

_____

_____

_____

_____

_____

What are some of the subtle thoughts and emotions that you have entertained that are not life-giving to you that you would like the Lord to minister to as you continue to read this book?

_____

_____

_____

_____

_____

Perspective

Chapter 5

Facing the Fire

"John answered and said to them all, '...but One is coming who is mightier than I, and I am not fit to untie the thong of His sandals; He will baptize you with the Holy Spirit and fire.'"

Luke 3:16 (NASB)

Facing the Fire

Fire is a subject that appears in numerous places throughout the Bible and has become a subject that has fascinated me over these last ten years in this season of waiting. Let me ask you, when you think of fire, what comes to your mind? For me, a few things stir up: sitting in front of a lovely log fire, roasting marshmallows over an outdoor firepit, wood disintegrating into ashes, gold being refined into its purest form, etc. Interestingly enough, as I am writing this book, forests are burning all over northern California. Smoke is rising in the distance over the lake where I am staying, and the impact of these fires can be seen for miles and miles around. People are being evacuated from their homes, and the threat of losing all their possessions becomes more real with each passing day. Whether you are envisioning a small burning fire under a mantlepiece or ravaging flames turning green life into ashes, fire is something we cannot ignore in our daily life.

My awareness of how significant the role of fire was in the life of a believer started in 2011 as I sought the Lord for wisdom and understanding during this time of waiting. After receiving a couple of words from different friends about Shadrack, Meshach, and Abednego and their incredible story of being thrown into the fire by the king of Babylon's order, I felt the Holy Spirit leading me to read the book of Daniel.

Something about the way they supernaturally survived this encounter was being highlighted to me. So, on one particular afternoon, I decided to drive down to the beachfront in my hometown of Hastings. I sat in my car and read Daniel 3:8–30.

As the story goes, Shadrack, Meshach, and Abednego were eventually released from the fiery furnace with not one hair on their head burned.

However, I found myself confused as my eyes read each line of the passage, and very gently, the Holy Spirit said to me, "Jill, it is possible to come through this season of fire without any evidence of having ever been in it." I knew this was truth being revealed, and excitement rose up within me. I started to journal the revelation I was receiving. Page after page of truth came to light regarding the war that happens inside us when we come to face our own personal fire. It was at this point when the Holy Spirit said to me:

"War victims and those who survive on land after war find it difficult to live in abundance after the battle is over. The restrictive living, the rationing of finance and provision, and the removal of freedom cultivate mindsets of survival that die hard. I need you to teach people how to live in My provision of abundance that I came to give as if they have always had it, even though they may face decades of battle, spiritually, to enter their inheritance."

As I wrote down what He was doing in this season in my life, the significance and purpose of fire, and His invitation to experience the fullness of the fruit of it, I realized that the fire we sometimes have to face serves to refine and reveal us, not destroy us.

I then recognized that the perspective I had concerning my season of waiting was negative and that I had been processing my unmet desire for marriage as a sign that something was wrong or that I was somehow at fault. Reading this passage in the book of Daniel helped to radically shift my perspective from a "woe is me" mentality to a place where I could actually see that God was indeed doing something quite special and that He was very pleased with me.

We can learn a lot from Shadrach, Meshach, and Abednego. The main reason they were placed into the fire was because of their righteousness. They had not committed any major sin before the Lord, nor were they attempting to run away from their calling. No, instead, Shadrach, Meshach, and Abednego had chosen to honor their God by not bowing their heads to the golden image of King Nebuchadnezzar. Under great pressure to conform, these three men decided to stand firm regarding their beliefs.

Just as Shadrach, Meshach, and Abednego were considered righteous, we too have been made righteous through Jesus Christ. Thus, we are charged not to bow our heads to the idols of the world where comfort and selfish living are glorified. As we have consciously chosen to follow the will of God for our lives, the waiting period for certain promises to manifest has very much felt like a fire. In this season of delay, the heat may feel unbearable at times. However, there is a greater glory that awaits us on the other side.

God is inviting you and me now on a journey through the fire, not to harm us but to reveal who we truly are as His children reigning on earth. Will you accept His invitation?

Their Righteousness Stirred up Anger

The righteousness of these three men stirred up such anger within King Nebuchadnezzar's heart that he ordered for the fire to be made seven times hotter, killing even the king's guards who threw them into the fire just because they came near it. What an image this is of what is happening in the spiritual realm around us. As we choose to follow Jesus and live for His kingdom, demonic powers rise up to challenge this, and as difficulties arise around us, it can seem like a fire that has one intention—to destroy and kill.

> Yet the Lord is revealing that the heat and intensity of this season do not have to destroy or harm us.

While Shadrach, Meshach, and Abednego were in the fire, they were joined by a fourth person, who King Nebuchadnezzar said "had the appearance like a son of the gods" (Daniel 3:25). Many believe this is the Lord Himself, and what is significant here is that the Lord was with them and was present with them in the midst of the fire. In an environment that was intended to kill these men, the Lord was with them. Jesus says to us in Hebrews 13:5 (NASB), *"I will never desert you, nor will I ever forsake you."* The Lord is wanting you to know that He has the power to keep you as you walk out this season and allow Him to do what He needs to do in your heart.

As I have shared, the Holy Spirit revealed to me that it is possible for us to come through this season and have no negative evidence of having ever been in it. When these three men of God were finally brought out of the fire by the Lord, the very one who had put them in it, their bodies had not burned; not a hair on their head was singed, and their clothes had no smell of smoke. In fact, there was no evidence at all that they had even been in the fire. When we yield to the leading of the Holy Spirit and understand that His presence is with us daily, I one hundred percent believe it is possible to come through the fire of delay with no evidence of having ever been in it. No damaged heart, unhealed wounds, no subconscious mistrust of the Lord, no lack or loneliness, just a manifestation of His glory in our life.

Something that I find incredibly fascinating about the story of Shadrach, Meshach, and Abednego is that it did not just end with them coming out of the fire. They were promoted governmentally by King Nebuchadnezzar, who *"...caused [them] to prosper in the province of Babylon"* (Daniel 3:30, NASB). This king, who was king of one the most notorious empires the world has ever known, said, *"Blessed be the God of Shadrach, Meshach and Abed-nego, who has sent His angel and rescued His servants who put their trust in Him"* (Daniel 3:28, NASB). King Nebuchadnezzar publicly acknowledged their God because of their trust in Him, and they were honored for it.

Shadrach, Meshach, and Abednego had to face the fear in their hearts when they were commanded to publicly worship the golden image of King Nebuchadnezzar. Their resolve, which we see in verses 17–18 (NASB), was:

...our God whom we serve is able to deliver us from the furnace of blazing fire: and He will deliver us out of your hand, O King. But even if He does not, let it be known to

you, O King, that we are not going to serve your gods or worship the golden image that you have set up.

This was not a light resolve but one that came from a life of true intimacy with God. In the fire of delay, the Lord is developing our intimacy with Him as well as our understanding of His nature, which is the foundation for how we can walk through this season and come out with the glory of the Lord displayed in our lives. I want you to know that you are not randomly facing a tough time with no purpose and no end in sight. God is up to something! Many years ago, I made a resolve to trust Him, and it still stands to this day, and the same can be for you too. God can and will use the very thing that we think will destroy us to manifest His power and goodness not only to us but to the world as well.

Take some time to ponder on this fact because, as history has shown us over and over again, it is easy to be suspicious about the character and nature of God. And still, He has not changed, and neither has His opinion and desire for you and me. He will do what He has promised.

Since that day on the beach at Hastings, the subject of fire has fascinated me. I have been amazed to see that in two of the gospels, it has been recorded that Jesus would baptize us both with the Holy Spirit and fire. Unlike the fire in the book of Daniel, this fire is not a punishment. It is a promise. A promise that the very Holy Spirit who Jesus said the Father would send to comfort, counsel, and lead us would also burn in us like a fire that would consume everything in us that is not in alignment with His incredible love for us. I have learned to yield to this fire and allow it to burn in me because that which is consumed by fire becomes fire! This is what I want for you as well.

Gold, in raw rock form, is heated in order for the dross and impurities to bubble up and come to the surface to be removed. It is quite a beautiful sight to see gold in its purest form. However, without the fire, the impurities would remain, and there would be no transformation. First Peter 1:7 (NLT) reminds us:

> *These trials will show you that your faith is genuine. It is being tested as fire tests and purifies gold—though your faith is far more precious than mere gold. So when your faith remains strong through many trials, it will bring you much praise and glory and honor on the day when Jesus Christ is revealed to the whole world.*

So, you see, we are not being destroyed in this fire of delay, but rather we are being refined by it. In the end, this fire will produce an indestructible faith and will bring glory to our precious Savior.

What I want you to understand is there is a much bigger picture at work than simply walking through and overcoming tough times that feel like fire. Like the three men in the book of Daniel, you are being refined and trained for governmental authority in the kingdom of God—a kingdom not of this world but one that holds all the authority and power of Jesus Christ, who has called and chosen us to bear much fruit.

The Fire Joseph Faced

We will discuss more on the kingdom of God later, but I want us to have a look at one of my favorite Biblical characters, Joseph. I find his life story incredible. Here was a young man who faced the fire of betrayal and false imprisonment and yet, came through it with no evidence of having ever been in it. I remember being a little girl, sitting in Sunday school, listening to his story, and reading about him in picture books and my children's Bible, but it was not until I got older that I realized I really did not understand the type of character God cultivated in Joseph during his time of slavery and imprisonment in Egypt. While many of us will never have to go through this type of fire, we can see it as a pictorial analogy of what a lot of believers experience emotionally, mentally, and spiritually when they are going through the trial of waiting for promises and dreams to be fulfilled.

Have you ever wondered what went on inside Joseph's heart and mind the two years after he correctly interpreted the Pharaoh's cupbearer's dream? Before the cupbearer went before Pharaoh, Joseph asked him to remember what he did for him by putting in a good word to Pharaoh on his behalf. The cupbearer agreed, but release would not come immediately for Joseph. Two years after his interpretation, Joseph still remained in prison.

Many of us know Joseph's amazing story up to this point, being sold into slavery by his jealous brothers, bought by the wealthy Potiphar as a slave, and thriving in that place of confinement until Potiphar's wife wanted to seduce him. On rejecting her advances because of his righteous heart, Joseph was falsely accused and imprisoned for life. Yet, the favor of God was still on Joseph's life.

When we read Joseph's story, it is easy to agree that every weapon formed against him did not prosper, and the Lord was with him, giving him favor wherever he was. *However, let us remember that we are reading God's perspective in hindsight.* We do not know the torment or pain that Joseph suffered as he lived out his thirteen years of imprisonment, especially in those last two years as he was waiting for a person of influence to vindicate him:

"But when all goes well with you, remember me and show me kindness; mention me to Pharaoh and get me out of this prison. I was forcibly carried off from the land of the Hebrews, and even here I have done nothing to deserve being put in a dungeon" (Genesis 40:14–15, NIV).

Yet, the cupbearer did not remember Joseph at all. In fact, he forgot about him. Put yourself in Joseph's shoes for a moment and think about the inner journey he would have gone on. The hope that must have arisen in his heart when the cupbearer was restored exactly like he had interpreted, the feelings, and the inner dialogue of "Finally, Lord! This is Your divine opportunity for me to be released from this false imprisonment." I can see him lying there at night in the days and weeks that followed and his heart churning with expectation of being called before Pharaoh for release. Like in so many cases, days turned into weeks, weeks turned into months, and months turned into years.

Joseph's vindication would not occur until a full two years later. In hindsight, two years does not seem like a long time, but when we are in anticipation of something, two years is a long time for the power of discouragement, self-analysis, despair, and unbelief to get to work. Although Joseph had the gift of dream interpretation, he had no idea when his release would come. God did not give him this revelation. He was left in the dark regarding this matter. It makes me wonder about the types of internal battles Joseph had to fight. Did he still believe in the promise his dreams revealed? Did he still see God as faithful and good?

When our outside experiences seem to be completely opposite of the promise that God has given us, it is easy to doubt that the promise will actually happen. It is during these times that our faith is tested and the fire is the hottest. Any attempt to grasp for answers that will provide relief feels futile, as it provides only a temporary quenching. Hope quickly descends into despair, and the future looks grim. Does this sound like where you are? Are you questioning the reality of your promise, God, or even yourself thinking maybe you got it wrong? In the next chapter, we will talk about the truth of your reality and seeing things from a fresh perspective.

Reflection Questions

Have you ever considered your time of waiting as a fire that can refine you?

_____

_____

_____

_____

_____

Have you ever considered your time of waiting as a time of God training your character for what is to come?

_____

_____

_____

_____

_____

Write down the character qualities you think the Lord is building within you during this time of waiting.

_____

_____

_____

_____

_____

Chapter 6

Beyond the Fire

"When you pass through the waters, I will be with you; And through the rivers, they will not overflow you. When you walk through the fire, you will not be scorched, Nor will the flame burn you."

Isaiah 43:2 (NASB)

An Inner Knowing

When I listen to many believers during their time of waiting, they just know that there is something more than what they see before their eyes. They sense that God is doing something, even though it feels very slow. This inner knowing is "hope," and we read in Hebrews 6:19 that it acts like an anchor that secures the emotions and inner process in a place of stability when the waves of the circumstances around us would pull us out into deep overwhelming oceans. I believe Joseph experienced this, and it helped him keep his faith in God.

God's Perspective versus What We See with Our Natural Eyes

The more I have read over the following chapters in Genesis, the more I have seen the Lord lead me to glean the perspective and wisdom that He wanted to get across in the story of Joseph. Many times, as I read this story, I wanted to know what really went on in Joseph's mind, and yet, the more I read it, the more I saw that God had another perspective He wanted us to see.

We read over and over in chapters 39 and 40 of Genesis that the "Lord was with Joseph," "was kind to Joseph," and "gave him favor" with Potiphar and the chief jailor. Favor with the authorities as well as success followed Joseph from the time he was thrown into the pit and into jail. It did not matter how confining the situation was; God's hand was on Joseph, and he was given special responsibility.

Just like Joseph, God is with us and is causing us to prosper even in this season of waiting. Can you point to a place in your life where you see God's favor? Is it hard for you to see or sense that right now?

If so, you are not alone!

Genesis 39:21 (NASB) says, *"But the LORD was with Joseph and extended kindness to him..."* Boy, has this challenged me! Kindness? I have admired the story of Joseph all my life. Be that as it may, the circumstances surrounding Joseph did not look like kindness. In the time period Joseph lived, a jail in Egypt would be anything other than pleasant. The horrendous sanitation, the oppression, and the sheer vileness of the environment were enough to make any sane person begin to question the validity of God's promise. Not only this, but the conditions Joseph found himself in offered a perfectly "natural" reason to complain, get bitter, doubt, and even give up. *In all honesty, would this really have "felt" like the kindness of God?*

Why is this important for you now? Take your situation and the daily manipulation of your senses as you face the very opposite of what you have been promised. This can be a breeding ground for natural thinking and offense against God. Step back for a moment and look at the areas where you see the kindness of God in the small, even tiny things. Meditate on this for a while, as it will help to "shift" everything back into perspective, especially if you have been struggling with strong emotions of despair. It may take some time, but face this fire. Face it, and it will reveal who you are and what God is doing in you.

As I studied Joseph's story, I realized there was much more that God was revealing through the fire Joseph faced. God wants us to know that His perspective was not on the problem, but rather He was using "all things for good" in Joseph's life to train him to reign and govern on this earth. The same can be said for you and for me as we experience our own fire of delay.

Many times, over these last ten years, I have marveled at the goodness of God toward me and the favor He has shown me in so many areas of life: work with Transform Our World, financial freedom, and deep healthy friendships and relationships as well as a family that has been transformed by the love of God. Yet, in this one area of my personal life, I have been tempted over and over to judge my life based on the circumstances. The danger of this is that the soul will focus on the lack. It needs to be trained to look at the big picture perspective of what God is doing and preparing.

I have often wondered to myself, *Am I like Joseph two years after the cupbearer forgot him? Am I still operating with integrity and taking care of what I have been entrusted with?* I face these challenging questions with each new day, and I must make a choice just as do you—whether we choose to look at our circumstances and believe what we see with our natural eyes or whether we choose to see things differently and trust God in the fire is entirely up to us.

Qualified by Grace

The very culture we are born into and the way we are trained to live by our successes in education, finances, work, marriage, children, etc., can deceive us into thinking that if things are not going well in every area of our life, we are somehow disqualified from the grace and love of God. And yet, grace is the very thing we need!

One of my life passages can be found in Romans 5:17 (NASB), *"For if by the transgression of the one, death reigned through the one, much more those who receive the abundance of grace and of the gift of righteousness will reign in life through the One, Jesus Christ."* Very early on, I got hold of the fact that the glorious Holy Spirit was training me to reign on this earth with Him. Let me be clear; this is not about preparing me for a heavenly reigning when I die. No, this has been a process of me allowing the baptism of fire to reveal to me my righteousness in Christ and the abundant gift of grace, both of which are received by faith and not earned by works.

Facing the fire of this season of extended delay has brought to the surface the areas where I have been trying to earn God's gifts and promises. God has used this season to reveal His truth for my mind to be renewed about who He really is and, therefore, who I really am on this earth. I am not just a woman waiting to meet a man and have a family. I am being trained to partner in life with someone God has designed for me. I am to bring the kingdom of God wherever I go, destroying the works of the enemy (especially in my soul) as I aim for the finished line of discipling nations and spreading the fame of Jesus all over the earth. The same is for you. So, whatever it is you are waiting for in this season of extended delay, know that you are in preparation to receive much more than what meets the eye. This is a kingdom blessing with a kingdom assignment.

Did Joseph know when he first dreamed, in Genesis 37:5, 9 of the sheaves of grain in the field all bowing down to his sheave of grain or the sun, moon, and stars all bowing down to him that he would one day govern the most powerful earthly kingdom with his entire family bowing down to his governing authority? Very unlikely. The fire he faced for over thirteen years of his life was a training and refining of his faith and character. It was the fire that enabled him to reign in Pharaoh's palace. The Holy Spirit does His incredible work of training us for the very thing He has chosen us to do; we will all eventually have to face the fire. The question is: Will you yield to His refining?

God Uses Everything

"...you meant evil against me, but God used it for good..." (Genesis 50:20, ESV)

God's intentions toward us are always good:

"For I know the plans that I have for you... They are plans for good and not for disaster, to give you a future and a hope" (Jeremiah 29:11, NLT).

As seen in the life of Joseph, God has a purpose for everything, and He will use our trials to bring us to a place of blessing. So, sometimes, what appears to be the hand of the enemy is really the hand of God positioning us to receive His good. When we are experiencing what seems like a never-ending battle of waiting, this concept can be hard to get our hearts and minds around. There is nothing about this time that feels good, but we have been given a promise of hope and a future. Please understand that when I say this, I am by no means encouraging anyone to accept from God that which we know is a demonic assignment. I will address this more later, but for now, my point is to help us to see that God's perspective is much higher and bigger than ours. While we are stuck on the ground and see only what is right in front of us, God's view of things is from the position on His throne in heaven.

When we look at Psalm 105, we see God's perspective of what happened to Joseph highlighted to us, particularly in verses 17–21 (NLT):

Then he sent someone to Egypt ahead of them—Joseph, who was sold as a slave. They bruised his feet with fetters and placed his neck in an iron collar. Until the time came to fulfill his dreams, the Lord tested Joseph's character. Then Pharaoh sent for him and set him free; the ruler of the nation opened his prison door. Joseph was put in charge of all the king's household; he became ruler over all the king's possessions.

Psalm 105 is about God's mighty works among His people, from Abraham to Moses. Here, in verse 17, *the big picture perspective was He sent Joseph ahead of God's people to bring them into Egypt, thereby helping them to survive the famine, which would have wiped them out.* From an earthly vantage point, it would be easy to think Joseph's experience was the work of the enemy. As we see Joseph betrayed many times, enslaved, unjustly convicted, and then used for his gift as a dream interpreter, how could we not think this? However, in verse 19, we see it is the Lord who was refining Joseph's character.

This is an incredible story to meditate on.

Open your heart to allow God to give you His perspective on your situation and even on the big picture of your life. I want to encourage you to do this so you can avoid the pitfalls that I have so often fallen into, where I have judged myself and my situation by the prison walls and not by the promise.

Reflection Questions

Write down the words, promises, passages, visions, and dreams that God has given you about your life.

_____

_____

_____

_____

_____

How is God training you in this season to grow into all the promises He has given you?

_____

_____

_____

_____

_____

Where do you see favor and the kindness of God in your life on a consistent basis like Joseph? What could this be showing you?

_____

_____

_____

_____

_____

What new perspective could you gain from this season as you look at the daily struggle versus the big picture?

_____

_____

_____

_____

_____

Chapter 7

Developing a Single Eye

"For He knew all about us before we were born and He destined us from the beginning to share the likeness of His Son. This means the Son is the oldest among a vast family of brothers and sisters who will become just like Him."

Romans 8:29 (TPT)

Jesus as Our Role Model

Jesus is the firstborn among many brothers, and He demonstrated how to live as a manifested son of God on this earth by the leading of the Holy Spirit. When it comes to delay, seeing Jesus as your role model will help give a new perspective on processing what you are waiting for in this season.

First, we are looking at a Jesus who was familiar with our sufferings and circumstances. When He was on earth, although He was God, we see in Philippians 2:5–11 (NIV) that He walked and lived fully as a man, humbling Himself to be found in human form, and He lived fully obedient to the Father.

> *...have the same mindset as Christ Jesus: Who, being in very nature God, did not consider equality with God something to be used to His own advantage; rather, He made Himself nothing by taking the very nature of a servant, being made in human likeness. And being found in appearance as a man, He humbled Himself by becoming obedient to death—even death on a cross! Therefore, God exalted Him to the highest place and gave Him the name that is above every name, that at the name of Jesus every knee should bow, in heaven and on earth and under the earth, and every tongue acknowledge that Jesus Christ is Lord, to the glory of God the Father.*

This is why we are exhorted in Hebrews 12:2–3 (NIV) to:

Fixing our eyes on Jesus, the pioneer and perfecter of faith.
For the joy set before him he endured the cross, scorning its
shame, and sat down at the right hand of the throne of God.
Consider him who endured such opposition from sinners, so
that you will not grow weary and lose heart.

Do we see Jesus with our physical eyes? The answer is no, although at times He can and does manifest Himself to people. With the exception I just mentioned, usually we see Jesus by faith. We must use our spiritual eyes. Here is the full verse of Hebrews 12:1–3 (NIV):

...let us run with perseverance the race marked out for us,
fixing our eyes on Jesus, the pioneer and perfecter of faith.
For the joy set before Him, He endured the cross, scorning its
shame, and sat down at the right hand of the throne of God.
Consider Him who endured such opposition from sinners, so
that you will not grow weary and lose heart.

This is an incredibly encouraging passage for our hearts during times of waiting because when we fix our eyes on Jesus, we get God's perspective too.

The Holy Spirit, who dwells within us, the incredibly powerful, wonderful Comforter Himself, is teaching us to fix our eyes on Jesus. As the Holy Spirit does this, we find that the truth that the One who pursued us and authored our salvation is also the same Jesus who will bring us into perfection. What a relief! So, my friend, take the pressure off yourself and release what you *think* you need to do to make things happen. Jesus has done it all for us! As this revelation begins to unfold more in you, you will find that the following passage we love and know so well takes on a whole new meaning:

"...seek first the Kingdom of God and His righteousness and all these things will be added to you" (Matthew 6:33, ESV).

When you fix your spiritual eyes on Jesus, you will shift out of seeking first "all these things to be added unto me" to seeking *"first the Kingdom of God and His righteousness"* because you will understand that it is from this place where everything you need and want will follow. The good thing is you do not have to figure out how to do this on your own. The Holy Spirit will train you.

This kingdom, as we begin to unwrap it, is significant to us as children of God. As Jesus spoke of the kingdom of God, which is within you and me, He gave some insight that, if properly understood, will shift our paradigm regarding how we process our experiences. The clue to this shift is given to us a few verses before Matthew 6:33 in Matthew 6:22 (NASB):

"The eye is the lamp of the body; so then if your eye is clear, your whole body will be full of light."

Developing a Single Eye Like Our Brother Jesus

When it comes to delay, perspective is key!

Perspective is the vantage point from which we look at something. We have physical eyes that see the circumstances and the problem and spiritual eyes of faith that see into the realm of the kingdom of

God. As children of God, it is impossible to get a true perspective on anything in our lives without using our spiritual eyes of faith.

I want us to dig into this concept a little more because it does matter which eyes you use. Your perspective and the eyes you choose to look at your situation can change absolutely everything! If you rely on what you see with your physical eyes, you will process from the position of the problem. Contrarily, if you learn to see with the eyes of your spirit, you will process from the kingdom—a place where there is no lack.

We see this with Jesus. He was able to endure because, with the eyes of faith, He focused on "the joy set before Him" (Hebrews 12:2). Jesus was looking at the joy set before Him, not at His experience as He went to the cross. What was that joy? Among other things, I do believe our being reconciled to the Father was the joy set before Him. But the key that helped Jesus endure the cross was in His choosing the eyes of His Spirit to see this joy.

We, too, have a joy set before us. We live from where Jesus finished. As Ed Silvoso would say, "We are reclaiming on this earth what Jesus Christ redeemed on the cross." All of creation is waiting for the manifestation of the sons of God to bring His kingdom in all its power and glory throughout the earth (Romans 8:19). This means we are not judging by what we see with our physical eyes but by what we see by faith with our spiritual eyes.

The Eye Lets in Light to Our Body

The way Matthew uses the word "single" is interesting. Single means focused on the kingdom of God in the realm of the Spirit, not focused on the circumstances or the problem. We see confirmed through the ministry of Jesus in Isaiah 11:3 (NIV) that *"He will not judge by what he sees with his eyes, or decide by what he hears with his ears."* Jesus is our role model. He showed us how to live in the kingdom of God in the present moment, a viewpoint that will have a profound impact on the way we see and process our extended delay.

What is the opposite of single? Double. It brings to mind double-mindedness, which we read about in James 1. Double-mindedness makes us unstable. I certainly have found this out for myself. If we choose to look at the lack and, therefore, focus on the delay, the frustration will increase the fruit of confusion, emotional despair, and a myriad of other issues that will impact the body like depression, sickness, etc. If our eye is single and focused on Jesus and His kingdom, then what He has promised is before us, and the fruit of that is hope, excitement, and divine energy to continue the journey.

Jesus Did Not See the Problem

Second Corinthians 5:7 (NIV) states, *"...we live by faith and not by sight."* We proclaim this all the time, and yet, we are still heavily influenced by our physical reality, causing an unbelievable amount of pressure against our thoughts and emotions as we walk through daily life. As I mentioned in the chapter on the soul, we are trained in the pattern of the world from the moment we are born to judge the physical realm by our senses. We, as believers, can change this particular pattern of processing today.

Paul affirms this in numerous places in the New Testament, and it helps us because we can fix our eyes, like Jesus did, on what we see in the spirit realm. Rather than judging by our circumstances and the walls of delay we see in front of us, this new perspective will help us to endure our season of refining:

> *For our momentary, light affliction is producing for us an eternal weight of glory far beyond all comparison, while we look not at the things which are seen, but at the things which are not seen; for the things which are seen are temporal, but the things which are not seen are eternal.*
>
> 2 Corinthians 4:17–18 (NASB)

If you are anything like me, it can seem as though the current circumstances are more real than what we know in the Word about our future and His promises. The key then is to develop a single eye by establishing in advance, once and for all, where we fix our eyes and heart. What we focus on—the promises that may not yet be seen—has divine power, as Peter says in his first epistle. In Hebrews 12:2, the word "fix" is the Greek word *aphorao,* which can be translated as "to look away from all else." So we could read the passage like this, "Looking away from your circumstances and instead fixing your gaze upon Jesus, who for the joy set before Him endured the cross."

As I have previously mentioned, we cannot see Jesus with our physical eyes, but by faith, we can. The same goes for the promises and vision God has set in our hearts. What seems like a delay and an extended waiting period then takes on a different meaning and focus. Instead of being something sent to discourage us, we become resilient to the attacks against our senses and, therefore, our souls.

Before we discuss this further, let me share a testimony about the power of fixing our eyes on Jesus, the Author and the Perfecter of our faith.

A Testimony on Fixing Our Eyes on Jesus

Back in 2016, I was on a day trip to San Francisco with a friend who was in town. We were sitting at my favorite coffee shop, Peets. Initially, the conversation started with us talking about what we needed to do to see things change in our lives, as there was a sense of hopelessness wanting to grip my emotions. Then, out of nowhere, right in the middle of our conversation, my friend blurted out, "When is the blood of Jesus simply enough?" Our entire discussion shifted from being focused on us to being focused on Jesus and what He accomplished on the cross. We quickly realized just how powerful simply believing in Jesus is! The atmosphere that had been rather heavy and gloomy beforehand had completely changed. For the next half hour, my friend and I joyfully conversed over this topic. At one point, I felt the most incredible tingling in my body as we locked eyes and boasted about Jesus. It was moving; it was powerful, and it was true. Jesus *is* enough.

Jesus is the "way" for us to walk, the "truth" for us to stand upon, and the "life" for our souls to thrive right now! What happened next is what has stayed with me ever since as a reminder to bring my eyes back to being "fixed" on Him and not my circumstances. I knew we would be leaving soon, so I got up from the table to buy half a pound of coffee. As I approached the cash register, even though I could not put my finger on it, I could tell something was different in the atmosphere. The young cashier with a lovely demeanor asked me what I wanted. I asked for half a pound of ground French roast and handed him my credit card, to which he responded, as he handed me back my credit card, "This one is on me," and, with a sweet smile, he took a card attached to his belt and swiped it. Now, I know you might be thinking, *This is a classic case of a guy just offering to buy a single woman coffee.* In the natural, it is easy to see this situation in this light, but spiritually, I knew something different was happening. It felt quite surreal. While I was waiting for my coffee, my friend came to join me, and I said to her, "Wow, here we are boasting about Jesus and the price he paid for us, and here I am getting something that I have not paid for. This is grace at work here!"

When the young man came back, with a jolly smile, he handed me not just half a pound of coffee but a whole pound, to which my friend and I agreed together, "Not only do I get something I didn't pay for, but I get a double portion of what I asked for. How Jesus is that!" As we walked away from the cashier with big smiles on our faces, I saw the next lady customer handing him a credit card, which he swiped. So I knew this moment had been a setup by God.

When Jesus became the single focus, the answer to our deepest needs and wants, and the focus of our praise, the atmosphere shifted around us. Through this experience at the coffee shop, the Holy Spirit has taught me a profound truth that I have gone back to several times since then when I find myself considering the problem above Jesus.

Are You Looking at the Natural or Spiritual Realm?

Now that we have looked at what is meant by the eye being single, let us look at how it impacts filling the entire body with light:

"The light of the body is the eye: if therefore thine eye be single, thy whole body shall be full of light. But if thine eye be evil, thy whole body shall be full of darkness. If therefore the light that is in thee be darkness, how great is the darkness!" (Matthew 6:22–23, KJV)

As a sports therapist, by training, I learned that the main focus of health professions is on psychoimmunology—the study of the connections between the mind and the immune system. Anxiety is a major cause of all illnesses according to many studies from the world's leading universities. Trillions of dollars globally are being sown into research to try to understand this, and yet, we, as believers in Jesus Christ, have at the tip of our fingers wisdom from the Word.

Our psyche is affected by what we look at, thus contributing to the healthiness or unhealthiness of our bodies. When we focus on our problems rather than Jesus, we jeopardize our health and open the door to a host of physical issues we were never intended to experience. Shifting back and forth between the natural perspective and the spiritual perspective does not help either. As we discussed earlier, this is double-mindedness, and it is destabilizing—not just spiritually but mentally, emotionally, and physically as well.

In the first chapter, I shared how I can sometimes get triggered by my circumstances because of what I look at. When my focus shifts off the truth of God's promises for me, off what Jesus has told me, off what the Holy Spirit has revealed to me, and onto the earthly evidence of delay and unanswered prayer, it impacts my thoughts and emotions heavily. As a result, I begin to entertain lies, which, in turn, cause me a great deal of stress, but no more! I am passionate about doing something about this and processing my circumstances through the spiritual realm—the way God originally intended for us to see things.

I want to point out something very important about the passage previously mentioned. It says, "if your eye is evil," but this is not referring to us being evil. What it is saying is that the source of our perspective matters. If we process from the physical realm, then we are receiving information from the Tree of Knowledge, which will cause our bodies to break down. This is one of the reasons why we are called to receive information from the Tree of Life.

The anxiety and stress caused by processing from the problem will negatively impact our health in more ways than you may realize.

As a person who is passionate about wellness, this is an area I want to see people achieve victory in.

Isaiah 11—How to Use Your Spiritual Eyes of Faith Instead of Your Physical Eyes

So let us look at how you can practically cultivate this as a lifestyle like Jesus did. First, make an inner stand to let the Holy Spirit teach you to develop a single eye. Like Jesus in Isaiah 11:3, do not make your decisions or judge by what you see with your physical eyes nor by what you hear with your physical ears. But instead, see what your heavenly Father is doing and process and act from there:

"Truly, truly, I say to you, the Son can do nothing of Himself, unless it is something He sees the Father doing; for whatever the Father does, these things the Son also does in like manner" (John 5:19, NASB).

> When Jesus came across a sick or demonized person or even a person in desperate need, He did not use what He saw with His physical eyes or heard with His physical ears as His source of decision making. His eyes were on what the Father was seeing and doing.

In the realm of God's kingdom, there is no sickness, no death, no lack, no poverty. Jesus understood this, which is why when the infirm came to Him, He saw them as healthy. He did not see leprosy; He saw the man whole. He did not see a man demonized with a legion of demons. Jesus saw what the Father showed Him about this man's destiny, about being free from oppression, and He simply called it out. This shift in the way we see things is essential for us to get, especially when we are in a season of waiting.

Second, it is important for us to realize that, in Isaiah 11, Jesus is not just talking about judging our circumstances, but He is also talking about not judging ourselves. This is where I have fallen into the trap of looking at my circumstances and judging myself based on what I currently see. The first few years into waiting on God's promise about marriage, judging myself in this manner was not an issue.

Now, twenty years later since that promise was made, the pressure to do this is much greater. Can you relate? In 2 Corinthians 5:16 (NIV), Paul gives us a strong exhortation to not judge others or ourselves:

"So from now on we regard no one from a worldly point of view. Though we once regarded Christ in this way, we do so no longer."

When I look at my situation with my spiritual eyes, I see a kingdom marriage and family, with children brought up to be led by the Holy Spirit and live for His kingdom. To see my life this way, even though nothing in the physical has changed, means so much. As believers, our focus has to be on Jesus and the spiritual realm of God's kingdom and not on this physical world. What do you need to resolve in your heart that will help you process your life through the spiritual realm of God's kingdom rather than the physical reality of your circumstances?

As you think about it, here is my prayer for you and me:

I pray that the eyes of our hearts may be enlightened so that we will know what the hope of His calling is, what the riches of the glory of His inheritance in us and the saints are, and what the surpassing greatness of His power toward us who believe is. These are in accordance with the working of the strength of His might, which He brought about in Christ when He raised Him from the dead and seated Him at His right hand in the heavenly places, far above all rule and authority and power and dominion and every name that is named, not only in this age but also in the one to come, amen.

Reflection Questions

Write down how you would describe being single-minded (single-eyed) during this time of waiting.

_____

_____

_____

_____

Write down some of the ways you may have become double-minded as you looked at both the spiritual truth and the natural reality of your problem.

_____

_____

_____

_____

What are some of the things you can do to practice looking at your situation through your spiritual eyes in order to gain God's perspective?

_____

_____

_____

_____

_____

Like a pregnant mother waiting expectantly for her baby, what is the joy set before you that you can fix your eyes on?

_____

_____

_____

_____

_____

Chapter 8

Timing from God's Perspective

*"My life, my every moment, my destiny—it's all in Your hands.
So, I know You can deliver me..."*

Psalm 31:15 (TPT)

Timing from God's Perspective

We live in the confines of what we call *kronos*, time, dictated by the sun and the moon. However, God is Spirit and exists outside this restrictive sense of time. With this being said, I want to show you how, through the life of Jesus, the Father's goodness toward us is not limited to time as we know it and how we can use it to settle our heart and mind on His true intent toward us.

Let us take a look at the story of Jairus' daughter in Mark 5:21–42. There was a delay between when Jairus first told Jesus his daughter was seriously sick to when Jesus arrived at his house to heal her. To paint the picture more accurately, Jairus' daughter was at the point of death, and, like any good parent, her father was desperate to save her young life. However, Jesus was in no rush at all to heal this little girl. We read about Him passing through a crowd of people.

Basically, He took the scenic route to get to Jairus' house. It is at this point in the story that we find out about the lady with the issue of blood. She was one of the people in the crowd this day, and in her own desperation, she touched Jesus. This was the touch that changed her life forever and all because Jesus decided to take the long way to Jairus' house. Can you believe it!

I have often marveled at this story. Here we have a dying girl at home and a woman in a crowd who is on the brink of death herself until she reaches out to Jesus. With just one touch, she is healed, and her life is spared, but this woman's story is unique. She stopped Jesus in His tracks because of her faith in who she knew Him to be. After she touched Him, Jesus became aware that virtue was leaving Him. An interaction begins between Him and this woman. Meanwhile, Jairus was trying to escort Jesus to his house so his daughter could be saved. I can only imagine how Jairus felt at this moment.

It appears as though Jesus was only concerned about this woman and had completely forgotten about Jairus' daughter. To add insult to injury, someone else got the very thing that Jairus was praying for his daughter to receive. Ouch! Have you ever been in a situation where you pray to God over a problem, and you notice those around you receive the very thing you have been waiting for? Maybe you are feeling like this right now. At the moment, life does not seem fair, and it is as if you are on the receiving end of a cruel joke. However, is this the truth?

Let us continue with the story. While Jesus was taking His time speaking with this woman, we find out Jairus' daughter died:

"While He was still speaking, they came from the house of the synagogue official, saying, 'Your daughter has died; why trouble the Teacher anymore?'" (Mark 5:35, NASB)

Can you see what is happening here?

Naturally, Jairus was probably thinking, *It's too late! It's not possible anymore! The opportunity has passed!* However, look at Jesus' reply to the news of Jairus' daughter's passing: *"Do not be afraid any longer, only believe"* (Mark 5:36, NASB).

What was Jesus highlighting here? Only believe. We then read on to find that even though He did not make it to Jairus' house in time before his daughter died, Jesus ended up waking her up as if she had just been asleep. Fascinating, is it not?

Now, in light of where you are on your journey, I want you to meditate on this for a moment: You are holding your desire or whatever it is you are waiting for in your hands in front of you. Imagine coming before Jesus like Jairus did and you receive confirmation that He will come to your house and answer your request. You know He can do it. He has put this hope within your heart, and it is yours by faith. And then time passes; life carries on, and you see others receive what you desired and requested. Like Jairus, someone else is seeing this goodness of Jesus in their lives. At one point, you felt so certain that you would get it, and now, with time passing, it looks less and less possible. The external words of doubt attempt to creep into your mind, "Don't trouble Jesus anymore. It's too late anyways." Does this sound familiar? How does it make you feel about Jesus?

Hurt? Disappointed? Angry? Fearful? How does it make you feel about yourself? Does it make you question what you originally heard or received as a promise?

Now hear these words, "(add your name), do not be afraid any longer, only believe." These words hold life in them, a power that transcends you and brings His resurrection life into your heart. They lift you high above what you see with your physical eyes to see His intent, His goodness, and that He is not limited to time. Mark 9:23 (NLT) says, *"All things are possible if a person believes."* Believes in what? In Him, in His nature, in the Father—He came to reveal. The Holy Spirit who dwells within you affirms this as the spirit of truth, and you feel a freedom from the constraints of the facts on your mind and emotions. Instead, the hope that does not disappoint rises up. All the passages that you know are true come together like a beautiful tapestry, and though you do not know how, you know He will, and this is what matters most.

I encourage you to stay in this place. Let the Holy Spirit stir up a response to your Lord, to your Jesus. It is here in this place of simple faith that the impossible becomes possible. You are not forgotten; you are not second best; you are not being punished. You are simply His, and He is coming to your house and will fulfill what He has promised.

Lazarus: Building a Framework of Belief

Another time when Jesus was late in the natural realm was when His good friend Lazarus died.

Once again, when it seemed like all hope was lost, Jesus used it as an opportunity for the miraculous to happen and the glory of God to be experienced. When Lazarus was raised up from the dead, *"Jesus looked her [Martha] in the eye. 'Didn't I tell you that if you believed, you would see the glory of God?'"* (John 11:40, MSG).

Lazarus had been dead for four days, which by the Jewish tradition was deemed beyond the period of resurrection. It was an impossibility to them as a culture, and so when Jesus originally arrived in Bethany and greeted Martha and Mary, these close and dear friends of Jesus had no framework for anything other than being comforted by Jesus. Comfort in itself is not bad. In fact, comfort from Jesus was what their hearts needed, but it was less than what He wanted to give to them. However, they simply had no framework for the supernatural here, let alone for resurrection from the dead. For example, when Jesus said to Martha, *"Your brother will rise again"* (John 11:23, NASB), she received His words as a reference to her brother rising again in the last day, but not right then.

Yet, it is now, in the waiting, where we can build what I call "a framework of belief." Years ago, when I started to receive the revelation of this refining season of delay, I knew that building a framework of belief was important to hang the revelations He would give me from His Word. Without this framework, I realized it would have been extremely easy to receive the comfort I needed by being in the presence of the Lord, like Mary and Martha, but not actually believing in the right-*now* reality of His resurrection power.

To help me build upon my framework of belief, I started to read the Word with a focus on God's character and the intent of Jesus while He was on this earth. So even though I did not yet see the manifestation in the natural, hope was being anchored in my heart relationally with Him because it did not change the truth that Jesus' intent and His desire was for me to "believe" so that I, too, would see the glory of God in my life. My exhortation to you, as you read this, is that you learn to build a framework in your soul that comes from saturating it in the spiritual habitation of truth. This truth is what you read in the Word of God, be it from meditating on the Word or praying in the Spirit about Jesus' intent and the nature of the Father He came to reveal.

We will cover the nature of the Father in more detail a bit later, but, for now, I want you to pay attention to your response when you read the incredible miracles in the gospels. See if you simply just pass them over as *That was nice for them. Jesus doesn't operate like that now; just look at me for that!* or *Why would He do that for me?* These thoughts are simply flags that highlight our soul's inability to receive in this area. For me, they can arise as a feeling of subtle offense against what I am reading. This is where I will intentionally allow my spirit to rise up and take the truth of what I read, and I saturate my mind and emotions in truth. Before I know it, I am getting revelation; my mind is being enlightened with fresh knowledge; my heart is being anchored in hope; peace is flowing within me like a river. I get excited about the possibilities all over again!

Tradition Can Limit Our Seeing His Real Intent for Us in Times of Delay

Let me show you how I realized tradition could be a limitation when I spent time in John 11. When I first read it, it seemed like a lovely story, but something rose up as an offense within me when I came to the part of Lazarus being sick and Jesus deliberately waiting to come to his friend until he had been dead for four days. I was so aware of the response within me that I sat there, opening my heart up. I asked the Lord to help me keep my heart soft and to show me what His intent was.

Going over the story again and again, I attempted to put myself in the picture with Martha and Mary.

Knowing they had no expectancy that Jesus could or would raise their brother, they could only receive His incredible presence and comfort. They did not realize that the presence of Jesus came to them for a demonstration of God's power in the impossible.

> Tradition and religion limited their ability to see what Jesus was really wanting to give them.

I then had to ask myself, "What religious framework do I have that is limiting me too? Limiting my expectancy?" Once again, I had been looking at the desires and promises with my natural eyes when Jesus was trying to get me to see that His deliberate delay was connected to the revealing of the glory of the Father. What was an offense started to shift to anticipation that delighted me because I knew I could receive this for myself.

This can be the same for you. I encourage you to open your heart and allow Him to speak to you beyond your current framework of tradition and religion. He *is* the resurrection and the life. Delay is not a barrier for Him, not even death!

Reflection Questions

Time looks different from God's perspective. What in particular has spoken to you in this chapter about God's timing?

_____

_____

_____

_____

_____

Read John 11. Allow the Holy Spirit to highlight parts to contemplate. In regards to what you are facing in this season, what truth can you begin to believe concerning Jesus' intent toward you?

_____

_____

_____

_____

_____

Can you see how your framework of time and delay can be preventing you from seeing His hand during this season in your life?

_____

_____

_____

_____

_____

Do you see the area of delay in your life as a weakness in your life or as an opportunity for the glory and grace of God to be received?

_____

_____

_____

_____

_____

Timing from God's Perspective

How can you apply a new perspective to your life now?

_____

_____

_____

_____

_____

Chapter 9

Receiving through Believing

"Therefore, I say to you, all things for which you pray and ask, believe that you have received them, and they will be granted to you."

Mark 11:24 (NASB)

Receiving through Believing

Can you see why believing is so important and why the enemy would go after this? If he can make you doubt that God really cares or is interested in your life on this level, you will settle for less than what He paid for on the cross. It is easy when we are facing delayed promises to process as if something is wrong, causing us to then start to act in our own strength.

Or worse, we let go of the promise and settle for less because it feels like God's grace is not sufficient in that area of life.

I have been tempted so many times to doubt and to settle, and each time He takes me back to His messages on faith, belief, and the issues of the soul when dealing with disappointment. Hebrews 3, in particular, speaks clearly about this issue. Although the Israelites had walked through the incredible, supernatural experience of deliverance from their Egyptian captors, they were characterized, in Hebrews 3:12, as having an "evil heart of unbelief" that prevented them from entering into the promised land.

Here is a closer look at how this relates to us during times of waiting:

> *Take care, brethren, that there not be in any one of you*
> *an evil, unbelieving heart that falls away from the living*
> *God. But encourage "yourselves" [heautous] day after day,*
> *as long as it is still called, "Today," so that none of you will*
> *be hardened by the deceitfulness of sin. For we have become*
> *partakers of Christ, if we hold fast the beginning of our*

assurance firm until the end, while it is said, "Today if you hear His voice, Do not harden your hearts, as when they provoked Me."

For who provoked Him when they had heard? Indeed, did not all those who came out of Egypt led by Moses? And with whom was He angry for forty years? Was it not with those who sinned, whose bodies fell in the wilderness? And to whom did He swear that they would not enter His rest, but to those who were disobedient? So, we see that they were not able to enter because of unbelief.

Hebrews 3:12–19 (NASB)

The phrase "evil, unbelieving heart" may conjure up some ideas of being demonic, but actually, the word for "evil" here is the Hebrew word *poneros,* which comes from the root word *ponos,* meaning "pain-ridden" or "troubled." So the emphasis is on woundedness rather than demonic activity.

> The warning here is that wounded hearts can be easily hardened, thus affecting our ability to believe and stand firm in faith to receive the promises God has given us.

This was the issue for the Israelites. As a result, those who had experienced deliverance from Egypt were not able to enter the promised land because of their unbelief. When the twelve spies came back from surveying the land of Canaan, only Joshua and Caleb said, *"We should go up and take possession of the land, for we can certainly do it"* (Numbers 13:30, NIV). The rest were full of unbelief and saw the giants that lived in the land as an impossible obstacle to overcome. In their eyes, there was no way they could defeat the giants and possess the land—their promised land. This natural perspective permeated the rest of the camp, and the people came into agreement that victory over this problem would not be possible—the giants were just too big.

Why did they believe this? Because the captivity of Egypt had wounded their hearts.

> Enslavement and captivity have a way of creating mind-sets that keep us living in survival mode.

Although the people of God had come out of Egypt powerfully and supernaturally, the woundedness from their lives in captivity prevented them from simply believing God would actually bring them into the promise.

It was not long after God's word to me about facing the fire when I read this story, and I realized how it was related. The miracles of the escape from Egypt, the crossing of the Red Sea, and the water produced from a rock at Meribah were not enough to heal the Isrealites' hearts. Before the spies even went out, God Himself told them He would give them the land! Look at what He says to Moses, *"Send men to spy out the land of Canaan which I am going to give to the people of Israel. Send a man from each of their fathers' families, every one a leader among them"* (Numbers 13:2, NLV). The men did not hear the heart of God when He said to them, "The land that I am going to give you." Due to woundedness, they only saw their situation through the lens of their natural senses.

God said He would "give" them the land, not that they had to take it by their own effort. Unfortunately, they just could not believe that God would simply give the land to them. If we are honest, we can admit we are guilty of the same thing. We struggle to believe God will give us anything without having to "earn" it first.

The writer of Hebrews says the answer to overcoming our woundedness is to exhort ourselves daily, which goes back to the chapter where we learned how to minister to our soul through daily exhortation and the creation of a spiritual habitation for it. I do want to emphasize something here. Our spirit is not wounded. It is our soul that is wounded, and it does not need fixing. I am well aware that it may "feel" like you are broken and damaged, but I have seen this over and over again. People who have come from backgrounds where it would seem impossible for them to ever walk in the fulfillment of joy and the fullness of life have grabbed hold of the grace of the Lord by faith and have allowed the daily ministry of the Holy Spirit to heal them. To heal our souls, we need to saturate our minds and emotions in the truth of what the Holy Spirit is saying to us *today*. This is how we can attain healing.

Beloved, right now, the Holy Spirit is speaking to you and to me. He is speaking words that can heal our deepest pain that no amount of soul searching can do. He is our Comforter and Counselor. He knows the workings of our soul better than anyone ever will. Sometimes His voice will be a powerful knowing within us, and other times, it will sound like a still small voice. Regardless of how the Holy Spirit speaks, His words will deliver exactly what we need.

When I do not know what to pray, I either pray in the Spirit or simply say, "Keep my heart soft, Lord," and then I listen to what the Holy Spirit is saying to my spirit. Following His lead, I am sometimes guided to passages in the Word. I have found that when I speak aloud the truth in what He has shown me, it always lifts me up to a higher place where I can see a different perspective. Each of us will be led differently. There is no "right way" or "wrong way." The key is to know that *today* He is speaking to you, precious one.

Faith Goes with Grace

We may think God is simply focused on the area of our desire, but as I experienced the revelation of receiving my promises by faith, I also found myself opened up to the full revelation of what grace really is and how it impacts our lives far beyond anything we can ever imagine. Many know it is by grace we are saved through faith, but it is also by grace that we live an empowered life in the spiritual realm and "receive" everything that Jesus paid for on the cross. Yes, this includes our promises. However, it also includes the restoration of His original intent for us when He gave the earth to Adam and Eve.

As I have walked through this journey of delay, I have become more aware of the emphasis of grace by faith in the New Testament.

In fact, it is a key focus of Paul's letters as he continually fought against the idea of starting our spiritual walk by grace and continuing it in works. It does not take faith to earn something through works, but faith is needed to receive grace.

So what exactly is grace anyway? I am glad you asked! When I was first introduced to the concept of grace, this is what I was told it stood for: "God's Riches At Christ's Expense." Maybe you have heard of this anagram before. Jesus, who was God, humbled Himself and came to earth in the form of a man to pay the price for our sin, for which death is the judgment. Therefore, He paid the price on our behalf. Anyone who chose to believe in Him would be back in relationship with the heavenly Father, saved from condemnation and hell. Because of Jesus, this person would now be able to experience heaven at the end of their earthly life.

Well, as wonderful as this seemed at the time of my salvation, I have realized over the years and, especially, being a part of an incredible body of believers in the ministry I work for, that grace is so much more. In fact, it is by grace that we reign on earth *with* Christ. It is by grace that we are conformed into His image daily and are restored to our original design! His kingdom is a kingdom of grace through the work of the Holy Spirit, empowering us to reign and live a life of victory over the devil and over all the adversity that we face. The beauty of it is that we receive *all* of this by faith!

We all start our walk with Jesus by grace through faith, and we continue in grace to receive the promises and the fulfillment of what He has for us. Why am I emphasizing this so much? Because very few believers actually know what they have access to in grace by faith and we can fall into working for the very promises Jesus said He would "give" to us by means of His amazing grace. John Bevere and his ministry, Messenger International, did a nationwide study back in 2009 with thousands of born-again, Bible-believing followers of Christ, asking them for their definition of the grace of God. Nearly everyone acknowledged the power of grace to save them, cleanse them from sin, and give them access to heaven when they died. Yet, only 2 percent said that grace was God's daily empowerment.

Second Corinthians 12:9 (NLT) says, *"My grace is all you need, for My power works best when you are weak."* Even though this was written by Paul, it is Jesus Himself who spoke it. The Lord describes His grace as His empowerment. So, if grace is God's empowerment to us to live a powerful life daily, then we are to access this empowerment by faith rather than attempt to earn it by works. The promises God has given you that you are waiting on have all been paid for. You only have to receive them by faith.

The battle the enemy is focused on is to either make you give up or to get you to try to make it happen for yourself. Taking either one of these routes will eventually lead to living disappointed, which is a much lower form of life from the one God designed for you to live.

Let me give you a good pictorial analogy of grace by faith that I heard. It really helped me make sense of what Paul said in Romans 5:2 (NIV), *"...we have gained access by faith into this grace in which we now stand."*

Picture this: You live in a town where there is a city water tower providing millions of gallons of fresh water, and there is a main pipe from the tower that runs along the front of every house in the town. There is no pipe that goes from the front of the house into the house. So, at this point, your home has no water.

How do you solve this problem? You get a permit and buy piping from the local hardware store, then connect that pipe to the main pipe in front of your house. Now, even if you have a fresh-water well in your backyard that you can use, odds are you would rather use the city system. Why? Because if your well runs dry, you will die. However, the source from the city gives you a limitless amount of fresh water. To put everything into context, I can say it is faith that serves as the pipeline of grace.

It seems so simple that the only way to partake in the empowerment of grace is by faith, yet many of us struggle in this area. Take, for example, Hebrews 4:2 (NASB), *"For indeed, we have had good news preached to us, just as they also did; but the word they heard did not profit them, because it was not united by faith in those who heard."*

The word "they" is referring to the Israelites when God was trying to bring them into the promised land. Unfortunately, they did not hook up their pipes of faith and tap into what the Word of God had promised them, not because they were not given access but because they had a faith paradigm based on works and not one based on God's freely-given, unmerited grace.

There is another element that must be discussed when talking about faith and grace, and that is *endurance*. Faith and endurance go hand in hand. Both must be present within us to fully see the manifestation of God's promises. If I can be transparent for a moment, the endurance part of this grace equation has not always been easy for me to do. I can say with certainty that, at one point or another, I was just like the Israelites Jesus was talking about. Thankfully, we have the Word of God to point us in the right direction so we do not disqualify ourselves from entering into our promised land. Let us look at some passages that serve to help us with this.

Hebrews 6:12 (AMP) encourages us to be:

"...imitators of those who through faith [lean on God with absolute trust and confidence in Him and in His power] and by patient endurance [even when suffering] are [now] inheriting the promises."

James 1:2–4 (NASB) reminds us to:

"Consider it all joy, my brothers and sisters, when you encounter various trials, knowing that the testing of your faith produces endurance. And let endurance have its perfect result, so that you may be perfect and complete, lacking in nothing."

The Greek word for "endurance" in Hebrews 6:12 is *makrothumia*, which also means forbearance, long-suffering. In the passage from James, the Greek word used for "endurance" is *hupomone*. This means patience and steadfastness. These two words depict what you and I are needing in order to come through the fire of extended delay unscathed.

We must remember that the acquisition of patience is a work of the Holy Spirit within us as we follow His lead. When we receive a promise from God, the Holy Spirit works in us patience as we are postured within our soul to receive and steward that which we have been freely given. This is the Holy Spirit's work from beginning to end.

Pregnancy is the perfect analogy to help us understand this a little better. A seed (a promise) is sown into the womb (our heart), and the grace of God grows and builds that child to full term. Expectancy is the posture of the mother's heart. Still, she is stretched in order to be able to birth the child at the right time.

For nine months, she waits patiently as every part of her body is stretched for the arrival of her promise. This is the joy James refers to—the eager expectation of what is to come. When we shift our perspective to this, it will change how we are experiencing this time of delay.

I see many times over that this is where most people get tripped up. Every time you are tempted to give up, to disqualify yourself, stop for a moment.

Refocus on the grace of Jesus Christ, bring your thoughts captive to Him, and gently allow this atmosphere of faith and grace to calm your emotions and stir up hope and even joy within you. Do not allow yourself to be discouraged. You have a promise that is on its way!

Reflection Questions

What response does the simplicity of the gospel to "only believe" stir in you? Do not be surprised or fearful of your response.

_____

_____

_____

_____

_____

Invite the Lord to meet you where you are. Remember He is greater than what is going on in your soul. First John 3:20 (TPT) reminds us that *"whenever our hearts make us feel guilty and remind us of our failures, we know that God is much greater and more merciful than our conscience, and He knows everything there is to know about us."* Write down your thoughts.

_____

_____

_____

_____

_____

_____

_____

_____

_____

_____

_____

How has your perspective on delay in the context of "patience" doing its work changed as you have read this chapter? What do the nine months of pregnancy mean to you in the birthing of His promises?

_____

_____

_____

_____

_____

Chapter 10

God Is Dealing with Us as Father

"Righteous Father, although the world has not known You, yet I have known You; and these have known that You sent Me; and I have made Your name known to them, and will make it known, so that the love with which You loved Me may be in them, and I in them."

John 17:25–26 (NASB)

God Is Dealing with Us as Father

If we fix our eyes on Jesus for any length of time, the heart of the Father will be revealed to us by Jesus. In fact, this was His number one intent while He was on earth. In John 17:25–26 (NASB), Jesus prays:

"Righteous Father, although the world has not known You, yet I have known You, and these have known that You sent me; and I have made Your name known to them, and will make it known, so that the love with which You have loved Me may be in them, and I in them."

For many years, I camped in John 17. It is so rich, and much can be gleaned from hearing Jesus' heart cry when He was under the most pressure on earth before His crucifixion. What is highlighted to me the most is that Jesus came to reveal God as Father, not God as Judge. He revealed the Father in what He said, what He did, and how He lived. Why is this significant? Unless we allow our hearts to be saturated in this truth of God being a good Father to us, we can fall prey to the facts that are before us, the negative news we hear, and the insurmountable troubles we face as evidence of an absent God. This will then lead to feelings of rejection and being offended by Him. As a result, we can end up spending our time either subconsciously trying to earn His blessings and promises or giving up because the work seems just too hard.

What I have noticed over the years in ministry is that most people, in some way or another, express that they know God loves them but are not sure He likes them. Another sentiment I get is that they know God is good; however, since they do not see certain evidence in their lives, they are not sure He is good to them. Although this is often not conscious, it is the same message I hear often from those experiencing seasons of waiting on the promises of God.

The impact of these subtle and subconscious perspectives affects how we process and, in turn, how we navigate this season. It can cause incredible stress and even health issues too. I want to show you how the soul and, therefore, even the body are impacted by a wrong perspective of God as Father.

Recently, I heard a message by a gentleman named Chris Blackeby called "The Still-Faced God," which speaks to this subject. He highlighted a study done by a well-known child-development psychologist, Dr. Edward Tronick, from the University of Massachusetts, who looked at how, even from infancy, an actual or a perceived "still-faced" parent impacts a baby's mental, emotional, and overall well-being.

The first part of the study is a baby responding to his parent who is interacting with them in a loving, facially expressive, and affectionate way. What we see is the baby will initially mirror back what the parent is doing with smiles, facial expressions, and warm responses. After a period of time, the baby will then begin to initiate new responses and will do actions indicating the discovery of the world around them by pointing to things and making new actions and expressions that show what they are wanting to do in the world around them.

Just like the baby in the experiment, when we, as children of God, are in that sweet, intimate connection with the Lord where we tangibly experience and see His warmth and affection for us, we mirror His affection and response back in worship, prayer, fellowship, thankfulness, passion for His Word, and a desire to know Him. We further express it in our outward activity with the world around us. For some, this is a regular occurrence; for others, not so common, but the key is sensing that God is expressing His love and warmth to us with us responding back. This is the foundational key for our mental and emotional development because it tells us, "This world is a safe place; I am wanted, and I can explore my place in this world."

What I find interesting and what I will be highlighting in this chapter is the part that comes next in the study. They asked the parent to then stop responding and become what they called "still-faced," and though the parent is present, they are non-responsive or emotive. What we see is, at first, the baby uses all his abilities to try to get his parent to respond in exactly the same way they had in the intimate moments beforehand—smiling, pointing and clapping, giggling, reaching. When the baby does not get any sort of response, we see him start to get stressed. He then increases his activity with a change in his voice and attempts larger reaches. The more time goes by without the parent responding, the stress response increases for the baby. At this point, the baby looks away from his parent, hoping to initiate some kind of feedback from the parent. What is also interesting is the baby will lose his natural physical posture and control of temperament as well. Due to the high levels of stress, the baby experiences a complete emotional meltdown.

Now, if we relate this to ourselves in times of waiting and extended delay where it feels like God is either holding out or just not interested, the process is exactly the same, relationally, with us.

> The same things we do in intimacy we will continue to reflect back to God in order to get a response like we had before. This is what we call religious activity.

This can include anything from prayer, praise, going to church, Bible study, and worship. Although these are good and righteous things in themselves, when they are done from a place of reaching for a response from a "non-emotive" God, they will cause incredible stress in the body.

When there is a deep suspicion against God and His goodness due to a lack of understanding of the Father and His goodness, the things we do to get God's attention will come from a place of stress and disconnection rather than from a rest response of affection. Even though the sense of God being non-responsive is a perception, our mental, emotional, and physical reaction is the same as the baby in the experiment.

Stress responses and trauma have been a huge subject, especially over the last ten years. At the physiological level, what we see when this happens is the amygdala in the brain, one of the brain's pain centers, fires more often, and we get what we call a "fight or flight" response. It is as if we are responding to a predator, an oncoming bus, or anything else that may jeopardize our safety. The fight response is similar to what the baby did initially when his parent went "still-faced." He reflected back on what he did in intimacy, and when there was no response, the baby reached more aggressively and made a louder cry but still remained in close proximity to his parent.

Early on in my journey, I did not know how to deal with my core perspective on my heavenly Father, so I experienced this feedback loop quite often. I would pray and spend hours awake at night analyzing and processing truth, including my actions and behavior, all in an attempt to figure out why I was not seeing an answer to my most precious prayer. When I could not hear or feel God, I would be sent on a tailspin in search of a response. I would go to events, read more, and reach out for inner healing and any opportunity to receive a word from others who could hear the Lord on my behalf. It felt like an endless and fruitless cycle of trying to get God's attention. I was emotionally and mentally drained. Does this sound familiar?

The second stage of response with the turning away and the loss of physical posture is the acute stage that leads to total meltdown. For us, this may look like struggling to read the Word, feeling numb inside, displaying anger outbursts, and blocking fellowship with Him and even other believers. What actually leads to us turning away is the emotional intensity that we feel at this stage. It is at this point that addictive behaviors can become the method to self-soothe. To be clear, I can tell you addictive behaviors do not always need to look like substance abuse, but hyper-religious activity can also be a way to self-soothe.

We are an incredibly complex and amazing species in the way the Lord designed us. We cannot remain at a level of heightened pain response, so we will find ways to come back to an equilibrium, even if it is temporary. Remember the emotional meltdown stage looks different for each person. So let the Holy Spirit highlight your coping mechanism. Without trying to fix anything, I just want you to simply become aware of it as we continue through this chapter.

One of the most well-known parables that Jesus shared actually shows how the wrong perspective of our heavenly Father leads to unnecessary stress responses. Many of us know the parable of the prodigal son. In my opinion, the title of that parable should be "The Good Father." This parable reveals so much more than just the journey of the prodigal son. Like the two levels of stress responses, we see two sons. We also see how their father responds to each of them and reframes their perspective about him. Let us take a look at this parable for ourselves. Here it is, Luke 15:11–32 from the Passion Translation, titled "The Loving Father":

> *Then Jesus said, "Once there was a father with two sons. The younger son came to his father and said, 'Father, don't you think it's time to give me the share of your estate that belongs to me?' So the father went ahead and distributed among the two sons their inheritance. Shortly afterward, the younger son packed up all his belongings and traveled off to see the world. He journeyed to a far-off land where he soon wasted all he was given in a binge of extravagant and reckless living.*

"*With everything spent and nothing left, he grew hungry, for there was a severe famine in that land. So he begged a farmer in that country to hire him. The farmer hired him and sent him out to feed the pigs. The son was so famished, he was willing to even eat the slop given to the pigs, because no one would feed him a thing.*

"*Humiliated, the son finally realized what he was doing and he thought, 'There are many workers at my father's house who have all the food they want with plenty to spare. They lack nothing. Why am I here dying of hunger, feeding these pigs and eating their slop? I want to go back home to my father's house, and I'll say to him, "Father, I was wrong. I have sinned against you. I'll never be worthy to be called your son. Please, Father, just treat me like one of your employees."'*

"*So, the young son set off for home. From a long distance away, his father saw him coming, dressed as a beggar, and great compassion swelled up in his heart for his son who was returning home. So the father raced out to meet him. He swept him up in his arms, hugged him dearly, and kissed him over and over with tender love.*

"*Then the son said, 'Father, I was wrong. I have sinned against you. I could never deserve to be called your son. Just let me be—' The father interrupted and said, 'Son, you're home now!'*

"*Turning to his servants, the father said, 'Quick, bring me the best robe, my very own robe, and I will place it on his shoulders. Bring the ring, the seal of sonship, and I will put it on his finger. And bring out the best shoes you can find for my son. Let's prepare a great feast and celebrate. For this beloved son of mine was once dead, but now he's alive again. Once he was lost, but now he is found!' And everyone celebrated with overflowing joy.*

"*Now, the older son was out working in the field when his brother returned, and as he approached the house he heard the music of celebration and dancing. So he called over one of the servants and asked, 'What's going on?'*

"*The servant replied, 'It's your younger brother. He's returned home and your father is throwing a party to celebrate his homecoming.'*

"*The older son became angry and refused to go in and celebrate. So his father came out and pleaded with him, 'Come and enjoy the feast with us!'*

"*The son said, 'Father, listen! How many years have I been working like a slave for you, performing every duty you've asked as a faithful son? And I've never once disobeyed you. But you've never thrown a party for me because of my faithfulness. Never once have you even given me a goat that I could feast on and celebrate with my friends like he's doing now. But look at this son of yours! He comes back after wasting your wealth on prostitutes and reckless living, and here you are throwing a great feast to celebrate—for him!'*

"The father said, 'My son, you are always with me by my side. Everything I have is yours to enjoy. It's only right to celebrate like this and be overjoyed, because this brother of yours was once dead and gone, but now he is alive and back with us again. He was lost but now he is found!'"

You can see the good loving Father at work in this parable despite both responses. We will return to this shortly, but first, let us look at the sons and see how they reflected the stress responses we looked at earlier from a perceived "still-faced" parent.

The first son I want to highlight is the second son we read about in the parable. We see here his response to his father is to remain close and try to reflect activity that would get a response from his father. However, there is a distinction to be made. His motivation was not from intimacy. The first son we know as the prodigal actually turned away from being in close proximity to his father. He lost control of any sense of mental and moral posture and squandered his inheritance on self-soothing activity. Neither son had the right perspective about their father, and they responded in different ways to the same issue. One said to himself, "I've been working like a slave for you!" while the other said to himself, "Please, Father, just treat me like one of your employees."

However:

> The father's nature was constant, and his heart of love
> and affection never changed toward both his sons.

We see this in the father's response to the son who returned from squandering his inheritance. He welcomed him and celebrated him as a son, even though the son came to him offering to be his servant. For the other son, who was upset that his father had chosen to celebrate the return of his younger brother, we see the father say to him, "Everything I have is yours." Essentially, reassuring his son that he had the same standing as his younger brother, who was being celebrated. There is nothing that he had that his oldest son did not have access to.

Even once the inheritance the so-called "prodigal" took with him was completely lost, there was more available to him. As for the one who stayed behind, although he responded to his brother's return with envy and bitterness, his father extended and continued to extend the invitation to come in and "return" too.

At the end of the day, nothing could ever separate those sons from their father's love and inheritance, except their having the wrong perspective about him.

I want you to reread the parable, but this time read it with your focus on the father. You will see there is no "still-faced" parent here. He is engaged and ever-present throughout the entire story. This is Jesus' message of truth about not just a father's love toward his sons but our heavenly Father's love toward us.

> The longer we wait on God's promises to manifest, the more susceptible we become to having the wrong perspective about Him.

Just like the two sons in the parable, our wrong perspective can lead to deep emotional hurt and feelings of being forgotten. The good news is we can heal from this trauma by having the right perspective about our heavenly Father, whose love and affection for us never changes, regardless of what we may think or feel. Take a look at these passages of scripture:

"Look with wonder at the depth of the Father's marvelous love that He has lavished on us! He has called us and made us His very own beloved children" (1 John 3:1, TPT).

"For I, the LORD, do not change..." (Malachi 3:6, NASB)

You may have turned away from God and distanced yourself from Him, but as the parable has shown us, you are never too far, and it is never too late to return home. The Father is waiting with open arms to restore you to your right standing as His child. His love for you is infinite and immeasurable. In fact, nothing can separate you from His love. Contemplate on this long enough, and you will be convinced like Paul in Romans 8:38–39 (NASB):

"For I am convinced that neither death, nor life, nor angels, nor principalities, nor things present, nor things to come, nor powers, nor height, nor depth, nor any other created thing will be able to separate us from the love of God that is in Christ Jesus our Lord."

The Holy Spirit is working in you now to convince you of the nature of your heavenly Father. He is committed to this, and so is Jesus. One of the last things Jesus prayed for you and me before He went to the cross was to make the Father known to us.

The Father does not have a "still face" when it comes to you or me. You *are* the beloved son in whom He is well pleased! "Beloved" means being the object of the Father's affection, and that is what you are right now in this very moment.

The Father's affection toward you is not dependent on your behavior, your history, or your earthly experience. It is simply due to the fact that you are His child. Receive this truth and allow the Holy Spirit to reframe your perspective of your heavenly Father.

Reflection Questions

How have your perceptions of the Father impacted your response to Him?

_____

_____

_____

_____

_____

Can you see how the wrong perspective of your heavenly Father can affect how you respond when you deal with delay and waiting?

_____

_____

_____

_____

_____

How do you relate to any of the responses of the baby to the "still-faced" parent?

_____

_____

_____

_____

_____

How can you lift your gaze off yourself to the nature and intent of your heavenly Father? How would this affect the way you process your current situation of waiting in your mind and heart?

_____

_____

_____

_____

_____

Chapter 11

Trained for a War You've Already Won

Then Jesus made a public spectacle of all the powers and principalities of darkness, stripping away from them every weapon and all their spiritual authority and power to accuse us. And by the power of the cross, Jesus led them around as prisoners in a procession of triumph. He was not their prisoner; they were His!

Colossians 2:15 (TPT)

Trained for a War You've Already Won

In 2016, I had a dream about the Father in heaven giving me a cup, and as He handed it to me, He spoke these words, "The Father's cup, trial or training." Immediately, when I awoke, I heard the words, "You choose!"

I knew the Lord was showing me that what I was going through was His cup presented to me, and I could have two very different experiences of it depending on my perspective. The challenge that He put forth in this dream was this: Was I going to view this season of extended delay as a time of being on "trial," or was I going to anchor my heart in the "training" that He was doing?

You may read the word "trial" and immediately think of James 1, where we are encouraged to consider it pure joy when we face trials of many kinds. While this is true, this is not the type of trial I am referring to here. I am referring to a trial that takes place in a courtroom where we are being tried and punished for bad behavior. If we are not aware of what the Father is doing with us, then we can fall prey to believing we are being judged like in a courtroom. Just like in Hebrews 12, with the good Father disciplining His children for their good, this is true for all of us as we wait on the Lord for promises to be fulfilled.

Just look at Abraham, who had to wait twenty years before the promise of his son Isaac would be realized. Joseph dreamed divine dreams of ruling thirteen years before his promotion as second in command of Egypt. Then there is David, who was anointed king fourteen years before he assumed the throne.

> The years in-between became the training ground for
> what these men carried in anointing.

Each of them faced their own giants: aging, prison, and Goliath. As impossible as their situation may have seemed, God was building them to be able to handle the *promise* they were given. This is the same for you and me! No time is wasted! Being aware of where we see God's favor like Joseph had in the prison with his administrative gift and our allowing the Holy Spirit to do His work will help us in the training process for what is ahead.

So where do we start? The kingdom of God!

Jesus taught the kingdom of God more than any other subject during His time on earth. This itself shows how significant it is for us to know and understand what and how it pertains to us.

> As children of God, we do not automatically become
> mature when we receive Jesus Christ as our Lord and
> Savior. We grow into it through the empowerment of the
> Holy Spirit, who trains us in the ways of God's kingdom.

These last chapters of the book have been written to shift your perspective on waiting and delay by revealing the truth of our heavenly Father and who you are. Be excited because God is growing you up!

"Train up a child in the way he should go; even when he grows older he will not abandon it" (Proverbs 22:6, NASB).

Training in the Kingdom of God

Jesus said in Matthew 6:33 (ESV), *"...seek first the Kingdom and His righteousness and all these things will be added to you."* This is what I believe Jesus wants to train us in, and for me, this has become even more clear over the last ten years. To go after and understand God's kingdom and His righteousness first, before all things, and then what we desire and need will be added to us sounds so simple. Yet, we often fail to do it this way. Our focus needs to be on desiring His kingdom rather than seeking to fulfill our unmet needs and delayed promises because when we do, all our issues are resolved. My encouragement to you is to read and spend time with the Lord going through the gospels and looking at the kingdom of God. There are studies you can get on the kingdom, but let Him bring revelation to you as you read what your Lord has to say to you. I am going to share a few things about the kingdom that He has shown that pertain, particularly, to delay and how the richness of what there is to receive is endless.

The Kingdom of God Is Not a Democracy

When we came into a living relationship with Jesus, we also became citizens of the kingdom of God. Like being citizens with a passport for an earthly nation, we are born into this kingdom at salvation.

Governmentally, the kingdom of God is not a democracy, which can be hard for many of us to grasp who have grown up and lived in a democratic society all our lives. There is one King, and He has set up the laws and legislations for this kingdom, not us, the people.

All Power and Authority Belongs to God Alone

The kingdom of God is the only kingdom with legitimate power. As shocking as this may seem, read these passages with me as I unwrap this. First, Jesus taught His disciples how to pray in Matthew 6:13 (NKJV), *"For Yours is the Kingdom and the power and the glory forever."* How many times have you prayed that prayer yourself? It does not say "a power" but "*the* power." There is no equal power to God and His kingdom. Then, after Jesus' resurrection, He said to His disciples, *"All authority has been given to Me in heaven and on earth"* (Matthew 28:18, NASB).

If Jesus has all the authority, how much does the devil have? The answer is simple. None! We read in Colossians 2:15 (NASB) that *"... He [Jesus] had disarmed the rulers and authorities, He made a public display of them, having triumphed over them through Him."* On the cross, Jesus won the battle for mankind to be reconciled back to the Father and to His kingdom, which contains everything we need. The original intent and design that He gave Adam to "rule over the earth and subdue it" (Genesis 1:28) has been restored to us.

If this is the only kingdom with power and we are born into it by faith as new creations, then we need to understand this kingdom and how it works to be able to walk and live in the freedom that we have been called to. You might be thinking, *If Jesus has all authority and has given it to us, then why does it look like Satan has so much power and authority? After all, just look at the sheer level of suffering on this earth!* This is where we come back to the first chapter on the soul and its significance while we are here on earth.

155

Satan does not have a kingdom, but he does have gates. Jesus spoke about these gates when He said, "*...upon this rock I will build my Church and the gates of hades will not prevail against it*" (Matthew 16:18, ESV).

These gates are anywhere where we see Satan has built a territory against the rule and reign of God's kingdom on earth.

As we have previously established, Jesus has been given *all* authority in heaven and on earth, which He has then given to us. And even though Satan has no legal right to our spirit, he can still deceive us. He will use our perception of our experiences to get us out of alignment with God. When we fall for the trap and believe the lie Satan has brought to us, he then uses our authority against us and the world we live in. Because of the fall of man, we are all susceptible to being deceived by Satan. However, we have been given the power to resist him when he comes to attack us, which I will cover in the next section of the book. Right now, all you need to know is that you are incredibly powerful. The omnipotent Spirit of God is in you, and, therefore, Satan has no power when it comes to the children of God unless we decide to give up our authority. *When we seek first the kingdom of God, it begins to consume our focus so that anything Satan is doing starts to come into its true perspective.* Instead of seeming so powerful against us and God's truth, it dims and fades into the background.

You Are Being Trained to See the Work of Satan from God's Kingdom Perspective

When we assign too much focus to the work of Satan, double-mindedness can arise. For example, how often have you struggled, believing the problem was bigger than Jesus? Or struggled with fear due to the intimidation of what you see before you and the message it is sending to you about how weak you are against what you are facing? You and I may know that nothing is greater or more powerful than Jesus, but it can certainly "feel" or "look" like maybe there are some things that are greater, which is why if we entertain this thought long enough, we get double-minded, confused, and frustrated.

There is a passage in Isaiah 14 (NIV) about the king of Babylon that also serves as a description of Satan. It is an incredible prophetic picture of him and how one day, we will be perplexed as to how something so small did so much damage to the world:

How you have fallen from heaven, morning star, son of the dawn!

You have been cast down to the earth, you who once laid low the nations!

You said in your heart,

"I will ascend to the heavens;

I will raise my throne above the stars of God;

I will sit enthroned on the mount of assembly, on the utmost heights of Mount Zaphon. I will ascend above the tops of the clouds; I will make myself like the Most High." But you are brought down to the realm of the dead, to the depths of the pit. Those who see you stare at you, they ponder your fate:

"Is this the man who shook the earth and made kingdoms tremble..."

The connection to Satan comes in verse 12, which should be translated as, "Oh how you have fallen from heaven, Lucifer (Helel), son of the morning, how you are cut down." In this passage, we have a hermeneutic principle at work here with a double reference about the actual king of Babylon but also Lucifer, the devil. Every day, he attempts to get us to believe the lies and accusations he proclaims against God and ourselves—believers and unbelievers alike. However, as believers, if we take these lies and accusations as our reality, allowing our minds to be transformed to the pattern of darkness, our authority is then used by Satan against us and everything we are connected to.

This is how double-mindedness works. I want you to take a moment and meditate on how you can maintain your authority during this time of extended delay. See what other scriptures and words the Holy Spirit gives to you concerning this matter.

Weakness Is Strength in the Kingdom

Here is a concept that is hard to grasp. Things that we "naturally" think are weak and foolish in our lives are considered wisdom and power in the kingdom of God. For example:

You have heard that it was said, "An eye for an eye, and a tooth for a tooth." But I say to you, do not resist an evil person; but whoever slaps you on your right cheek, turn the other to him also. If anyone wants to sue you and take your shirt, let him have your coat also. Whoever forces you to go one mile, go with him two. Give to him who asks of you, and do not turn away from him who wants to borrow from you.

Matthew 5:38–42 (NASB)

Why is this so hard for us to do? Because in the world we live in, outward strength, power in the form of success, and prestige are what we elevate. In this world, we do not rejoice in weakness. However, in the kingdom of God, we can. As Paul proclaimed in 2 Corinthians 12:9 (NIV), *"Therefore I will boast all the more gladly about my weaknesses, so that Christ's power may rest on me"* we must also see ourselves in this light. Remember the power belongs to Jesus Christ, who freely releases it into our lives by grace. In those moments when we feel vulnerable and weak, God's power shows up greatest in our lives. Do you feel weak today? Ask the Holy Spirit to minister to you by speaking a fresh word of truth and confirmation.

God's Word to You Has the Power to Produce
Exactly What He Promised

The words of Jesus are not just words; they are *spirit and life* (John 6:63). Let me give you an example. Matthew 5:36–37 (NASB) says, *"Nor shall you make an oath by your head, for you cannot make one hair white or black. But let your statement be, 'Yes, yes' or 'No, no'; anything beyond these is of evil."* One morning, as I contemplated this passage with the Lord, I was considering what it was saying for me to do, and I heard Him say, "Would I ask you to do what I Myself would not do?" This question opened up a new revelation that when God says yes to something in our lives, a revelation, a word, a dream, a desire, He is not going back on it. His "yes" is yes! To consider anything else is "evil." Some translations say "evil one." This is an incredible revelation. If God has said yes to your request, there is no need to consider anything else. Just believe and remain in God! Allow the Holy Spirit to bring forth the fruit of believing, which will be to the glory of our heavenly Father. I want to encourage you to read Matthew 5:37 in different translations and become intentional about resisting the temptation to contemplate on "Yes, but..." or "No, but...," which only leads to double-mindedness. Let the words of Jesus, which are *spirit* and *life,* become an anchor for your soul while you wait.

I have mentioned this before, but I will emphasize it again: Satan is not trying new tricks. They are the same ones he used with Eve in the garden. When Satan asked her, "Did God really say?" he made her believe God was holding out on her, and Satan is attempting to do it to you and me in this season of waiting. We may not have a physical being in front of us questioning God directly, but what we will get are thoughts. Most often, these thoughts present themselves in the first person. However, the reality is they are from Satan himself to make us question ourselves and God, *Yes, He loves me, but... Maybe I heard wrong...* Another way to uncover Satan's attacks is to look at any area of your life where you "feel" a subtle suspicion against God's goodness and His loving nature. Here, you will find seeds (words) Satan has sown, aimed to create doubt within you. Take a moment to contemplate this now.

The Kingdom Provides All You Need

This is an important issue to settle in your heart because, during times of delay, we can be prone to lies from Satan that keep us striving to attain something that is already ours in Christ and accessible in the kingdom. Everything we need is in the kingdom of God, and, in Matthew 6:25–34 (NASB), Jesus really stresses this point:

For this reason, I say to you do not be worried about your life, as to what you will eat or what you will drink; nor for your body, as to what you will put on. Is not life more than food, and the body more than clothing? Look at the birds of the air, that they do not sow, nor reap nor gather into barns, and yet your heavenly Father feeds them. Are you not worth much more than they? And who of you by being worried can add a single hour to his life? And why are you worried about clothing?

Observe how the lilies of the field grow; they do not toil nor do they spin, yet I say to you that not even Solomon, in all his glory, clothed himself like one of these. But if God so clothes the grass of the field, which is alive today and tomorrow is thrown into the furnace, will He not much more clothe you?

You of little faith! Do not worry then, saying, "What will we eat?" or "What will we drink?" or "What will we wear for clothing?" For the Gentiles eagerly seek all these things; for your heavenly Father knows that you need all these things. But seek first His kingdom and His righteousness, and all these things will be added to you. So do not worry about tomorrow; for tomorrow will care for itself. Each day has enough trouble of its own.

The truth here is you and I do not have to "sow and reap." In other words, we do not have to earn or strive for that which our heavenly Father freely gives us by grace. What do the non-believers run after? Food, drink, clothing, living space—all of these are needs!

In Maslow's hierarchical list of needs, these fall under the "basic needs" that we all need, and from these needs, everything else is built.

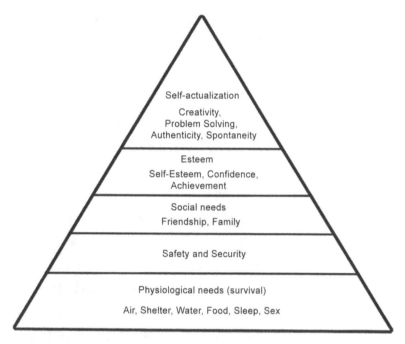

When Jesus said, *"...seek first the Kingdom and His righteousness... all these things will be added to you,"* what He was essentially saying was this, "Rather than striving and running after all these things first, do the opposite. Do not run after them at all. Just know I will provide as you seek first My kingdom and My righteousness." Remembering this will help us to stop striving even for the basic needs that He said He would provide. Another passage for us to remember comes from Romans 8:32 (NKJV), *"He who did not spare His own Son, but delivered Him over for us all, how will He not also with Him freely give us all things?"*

There Is a War, but We Have Already Won!

What we often fail to teach new believers when they are saved is that they have entered a kingdom, and this kingdom is at war, whether they want to fight or not. They will experience it. It is in the kingdom of God where we, as children of God, are empowered to take the dominion of the finished work of Jesus.

In turn, it helps us to overcome the domain of Satan in our souls, marriages, families, relationships, spheres of influence, cities, and nations. The kingdom of God is within us, and so this is where the greatest battle is.

The devil hates the kingdom of God, but it is important for us to know that the war with the enemy has already been won by Jesus. The *real* battle is standing in that truth and bringing it to all the areas of life where we do not see this manifesting—ours, those around us, our communities, cities, and nations.

Here are some passages to meditate on that will help you to see that even though we have entered a war, Jesus has paid the highest price for us to stand in a place of victory. Through His sacrifice, we have been given spiritual weapons to wage a battle against the works of darkness in us and around us:

"When He had disarmed the rulers and authorities, He made a public display of them, having triumphed over them through Him" (Colossians 2:15, NASB).

For we do not wrestle against flesh and blood, but against the rulers, against the authorities, against the cosmic powers over this present darkness, against the spiritual forces of evil in the heavenly places. Therefore, take up the whole armor of God, that you may be able to withstand in the evil day, and having done all, to stand firm. Stand therefore, having fastened on the belt of truth, and having put on the breastplate of righteousness, and, as shoes for your feet, having put on the readiness given by the gospel of peace. In all circumstances take up the shield of faith, with which you can extinguish all the flaming darts of the evil one.

Ephesians 6:12–16 (ESV)

Paul, the author of Ephesians, wrote the book as a strategy to overcome. He gives an exhortation in his letter that summarizes it this way:

"Finally, be strong in the Lord and in the strength of His might. Put on the full armor of God, so that you will be able to stand firm against the schemes of the devil" (Ephesians 6:10–11, ESV).

The devil is cunning, and if we are not prepared, he will have us off balance. This is why we are encouraged to put on the *full* spiritual armor of God so that we can remain standing when the devil's attacks come. You might be asking yourself, "What exactly is this spiritual armor that we have been given to put on, and how can we use it in this season of waiting?" Great question! Let us find out.

165

Reflection Questions

Does being trained in the kingdom of God seem different from being on trial for you?

_____

_____

_____

_____

_____

When you read, "...*seek first the Kingdom of God and His righteousness...*," how does this make a difference for you as you wait on the Lord for His promises to be fulfilled in your life?

_____

_____

_____

_____

_____

Jesus spoke about the kingdom more than any other subject. What has spoken to you the most in this chapter?

_____

_____

_____

_____

_____

Chapter 12

The Winning Armor

Then Jesus, overflowing with the Holy Spirit's joy, exclaimed, "Father, thank you, for you are Lord Supreme over heaven and earth! You have hidden the great revelation of this authority from those who are proud, those wise in their own eyes, and you have shared it with these who humbled themselves. Yes, Father. This is what pleases your heart: to give these things to those who are like trusting children.

Luke 10:21 (TPT)

Truth Sets Me Free, Not Knowledge

The battle is ultimately spiritual, so we do not overcome spiritual battles with the soulish/physical weapons of warfare like academics, head knowledge, guns, or knives. The weapons we use are spiritual, and 1 Peter says that they have "divine power." When it comes to living with the armor of God on us, we see that, in the kingdom, freedom comes from wearing the "belt of truth" (Ephesians 6:14). Jesus Himself said in John 8:31–32 (KJV):

"Then said Jesus to those Jews which believed on Him, If ye continue in My word, then are ye My disciples indeed; And ye shall know the truth, and the truth shall make you free."

Because the battle is spiritual and not tied to the soul, the power is not based on analyzing our situation with our minds, something we can so easily be drawn into. If anything, that just leads us into a pit of despair, and I want us to break the cycle. The more we contemplate the truth of the gospel of the kingdom, the freer you and I will become within ourselves.

This is also where I want to gently exhort you to accompany truth with grace. Have you ever had anyone tell you truth from the Word of God, and it felt more like condemnation than freedom? This is usually because it is not accompanied with love and grace.

The foundation of the kingdom is love. Anything that operates outside of this, no matter how true it may be, will not be received as freedom.

All the Darts Are Extinguished with the Shield of Faith

"Above all, taking the shield of faith, wherewith ye shall be able to quench all the fiery darts of the wicked" (Ephesians 6:16, KJV).

I looked up the Greek translation for the word "all," and it translates to *pas*, which literally means "all" or "every." So here we have the shield of faith that puts out *all* the fiery darts of the evil one. Not just a few or some—*all*.

What are the darts? The darts are the lies, the words, the accusations fired against us by Satan. The onslaught against our mind can feel like torment when we contemplate the reality of what we are facing and experiencing. Yet, the *shield* protects us from having to fight the darts. Practically, this looks like resisting the thoughts, the words, and the accusations that contradict the character and nature of God rather than entertaining them. This takes discipline. Thankfully, we have been given the truth and the revelation to know, so when accusations arise, all we have to do is simply lift up our shield of faith and resist.

I used to spend hours awake at night, contemplating and fighting for peace through a web of thoughts and arguments about my life. Once I understood that I had the ability to resist the darts, I no longer struggled as much to maintain my peace. We can waste so much energy analyzing what and why things are happening to us when we do not have to. We have been given a promise and the authority to protect that promise until it comes to pass. You and I have the choice to use this time in such a way that when we finally receive God's promise, we will be equipped for whatever comes attached to it. Remember this can be a time of trial or training. I choose training. What about you?

Your heavenly Father is committed to training you by the leadership of His Spirit within you. It took training for me to shift out of reasoning and knowledge, and you can do it too. Yes, the fiery darts will come. It is part of the battle. No one is immune. All believers experience the fiery darts no matter how good their life may look on the outside. What is most important is that you learn to hold the shield up for yourself instead of depending on others to hold up their own shield for you. This is what spiritual maturity looks like, and it should be a goal of ours.

The first step to learning how to hold up your shield is becoming aware of when you lose your peace. This is a sure sign that something is triggering you. Thoughts become feelings, and their power can be overwhelming. So pay attention to what you are thinking about. I always bring the Holy Spirit into this, as He can highlight one thing that will shift everything for me. As you yield to Him, be aware that the mind governed by the Holy Spirit is "life and peace." When you experience any destructive analysis that leads you away from the Lord rather than toward Him, allow the Holy Spirit to bring it to your awareness so it can be addressed.

Shields can be very heavy. I have picked up a few over the years in museums, shows, etc., and they are always heavier than you think. Training to have the muscles and strength to uphold a shield is important. As a sports therapist, many injuries I have dealt with over the years have come from people doing too much too soon when the body is not able to take the strain they wanted it to. I cannot emphasize enough what an incredible personal trainer the Holy Spirit is. He will be specific with you for what *you* need. The Holy Spirit will give you revelation as you read the Word and spend time with Him. This is what your faith is based on—the revealed truth to your heart. So know what you believe in your heart.

As the apostle Paul exhorts, know what you believe in your heart and watch who you give inner access to. I will admit sometimes we just do not feel like using our shield and are just tired of what feels like a constant fight. This is where I believe compassion is needed. We also need the understanding that we have been designed and wired by God to win the battles that we face, which makes our training incredibly significant.

Direct Combat

The sword of the Spirit is the only offensive piece of warfare we have. When I thought about this and what it would be like to use a sword with all I was facing, the first thing the Holy Spirit showed me was that the enemy has no sword or weapon to fight against me. Allow this revelation to sink in deep. As you do, take a look at Colossians 2:13–15 (NASB):

> ...*when you were dead in your transgressions and the uncircumcision of your flesh, He made you alive together with Him, having forgiven us all our transgressions, having canceled out the certificate of debt consisting of decrees against us, which was hostile to us; and He has taken it*

out of the way, having nailed it to the cross. When He had
disarmed the rulers and authorities, He made a public
display of them, having triumphed over them through Him.

Satan is disarmed. Yet, the reality of demonic activity around us can feel like we are facing a very powerful foe who is stronger than we are, but this is just a perception and *not* the truth. When we believe we are facing an armed enemy, we may be tempted to not stand and fight. Unfortunately, this is what I see many believers doing—backing down, settling for less, and living out of the realm of reasoning based on physical circumstances. That is not where the battle is! The battle is spiritual, but it takes place in our mind.

Second Corinthians 10:3–5 (NASB) teaches us how to use the sword:

For though we walk in the flesh, we do not war according
to the flesh, for the weapons of our warfare are not of the
flesh, but divinely powerful for the destruction of fortresses.
We are destroying speculations and every lofty thing raised
up against the knowledge of God, and we are taking every
thought captive to the obedience of Christ.

We can use the sword of the Word of God to destroy, from the root, any "mindset" or "stronghold" that is impregnated with hopelessness and has caused us to accept something that we know is contrary to the Word and will of God. It was Ed Silvoso who so clearly described this in one of his bestselling books, *Strongholds: What They Are and How to Pull Them Down*. Some things are more obvious than others, but they are all located in the mind. They are made up of good thoughts and intentions. They develop in the shadow of our strengths, are activated by trauma, detonated by crisis, and create double-mindedness that results in emotional and spiritual instability.

Once again, this is where we see the words of Jesus in Matthew 6 about the "single eye" play out because instead of simply believing the truth, the mindset or stronghold resists it, and we become double-minded.

Once a stronghold is detected, the sword is used in direct combat against the lie. The key focus is to not give up. Use your biblical arsenal of truth against the lie like Jesus did when He was tempted by the devil in the wilderness. Jesus used the Word of God against Satan's challenge. Although Satan used facts and even subtly twisted the Word to tempt Him, those words were not the truth the Father intended for Jesus. Jesus used the sword of the true Word against the devil.

Do not be surprised about the strongholds you will find. Jesus showed me in His parable of the sower how there is soil in our heart that both wheat and thorns grow in. It took me a long time to realize how many seeds of contention against the truth had been sown in my life through experience. Some of those experiences were traumatic, and others were just experiences in this fallen world. However, Jesus did say that when the time was right, they would be harvested together, or a better way to put it, *uprooted* together. Therefore, I am no longer shaken in the same way. Certain triggers allow strongholds to reveal themselves, which indicates to me that it is time for harvest.

I want you to also remember that although there are strongholds of the enemy in the mind, God, as well, has a stronghold. What is the stronghold of God? The mind of Christ! Get excited because this is what you have been freely given! Read 1 Corinthians 2:14–16 (AMP) with me:

> But the natural [unbelieving] man does not accept the things [the teachings and revelations] of the Spirit of God, for they are foolishness [absurd and illogical] to him; and he is incapable of understanding them, because they are spiritually discerned and appreciated, [and he is unqualified to judge spiritual matters].
>
> But the spiritual man [the spiritually mature Christian] judges all things [questions, examines and applies what the Holy Spirit reveals], yet is himself judged by no one [the unbeliever cannot judge and understand the believer's spiritual nature]. For who has known the mind and purposes of the Lord, so as to instruct him? But we have the mind of Christ [to be guided by His thoughts and purposes].

You have been given the mind of Christ! As we yield our natural thinking based on what we see and hear in the physical realm to the mind of Christ, our minds become renewed, allowing the stronghold of God to be built within our souls. Like I mentioned before, the soul was created for a spiritual habitation, and here, in the stronghold of God, we have that. I refer you back to the mold of the soul and what we are building and forming in our minds. What the enemy has done with the lies he has brought up cannot become what we fix our eyes on. It must always be Jesus.

We read in the psalms how much our focus impacts any battle we are in. My favorite psalm, Psalm 18, highlights so well how we are to see God during our battles. Here are verses 1–2 (NIV):

"I love You, O Lord, my strength.

"The Lord is my rock and my fortress and my deliverer, My God, my rock, in whom I take

"refuge; My shield and the horn of my salvation, my stronghold."

We are not just going after the lies of the enemy and combating them with the sword of the Word. We need a reference point of God's presence; otherwise, the battle is useless, and victory is impossible. The reality of our soul finding rest in God alone can be seen in so many ways in Scripture. Here we have David, a man after God's heart, describing God Himself as *his* fortress, *his* stronghold. In battle, this is where safety is found, and protection from the enemy is given, but this is also the place to battle from! So, remember, it is when we are in the presence of Jesus that the strength to overcome is manifested.

The Breastplate of Righteousness

This is a key piece of armor because we are supposed to never take this off. When I minister to people who are experiencing extended periods of waiting and delay, I find a common theme is located in the context of righteousness. On one extreme, we believe that we have done something to deserve the delay, and on the other extreme, we have not done enough to deserve the blessing and freedom we desire. Both of these are lies from the pit of hell.

Having the right perspective about our righteousness is foundational to us as believers in Christ. We are made "right" with the Father by the blood of Jesus Christ, and it is as simple as that!

Neither our right standing nor the relationship we have with the Father will ever change. Just because we are facing delay or what looks like unanswered prayers does not mean we are now unrighteous or out of relationship with Him. When I see this happening, I call it an illusion of separation. The Holy Spirit has ministered to me in this area more than any other area in my life because it is all about identity.

As soon as we get this, the rest falls into place. The breastplate of righteousness is what the belt of truth sits upon. You and I have a righteousness that came by faith. We do not have to earn it.

Trying to Get into a Room You Are Already In

I once heard someone say that when we, as believers, try to earn the blessings of God, it is like trying to get into a room that we are already in.

Instead of joy and happiness, we get frustration. This is because we are processing from a place where we view ourselves as separate from Him, and we need to somehow get to a place where we feel righteousness in order to receive what we are needing. My friend, it is in these moments that the righteousness of Christ, which is now ours, realigns our thinking and processing.

178

I cannot emphasize enough how fundamental this is. For years, I did many types of inner healing, yet I found that much of that came from this illusion of separation where I somehow felt "off," that I had missed my blessing because either He was not pleased with me in some way or I was not free or ready, etc.

Spend some time acknowledging your righteousness in Christ Jesus, thanking Him, and meditating on 2 Corinthians 5:21 (TPT):

"For God made the only one who did not know sin to become sin for us, so that we who did not know righteousness might become the righteousness of God through our union with Him."

Righteousness is what I have spent most of my time meditating on over these last ten years. It is where the words of Jesus, "It is finished!" have context because my identity is now grounded in the Father's heart toward me.

I want you to spend some time with the Lord and ask Him to reveal to you any mindset He is wanting you to deal with. Journal it and declare war against it.

Lord, thank You that all authority in heaven and on earth is Yours and that same authority is residing within us right now as we pray. We ask that You reveal to us any thoughts in our minds that are impregnated with hopelessness that have become a stronghold against Your truth and Your desire for us. As You reveal this, Lord, we acknowledge that You have armed us to overcome with You. We thank You for the freedom for which You have set us free. Today, we stand and declare war on any stronghold resident in our mind that You want us to deal with. In the wonderful name of Jesus, amen.

Reflection Questions

How does being prepared and equipped for the battle help you when it comes to living in the kingdom of God?

_____

_____

_____

_____

_____

How can this make a difference to you as you navigate the seasons of delay?

_____

_____

_____

_____

_____

Here are additional passages on your righteousness in Christ. Spend some time meditating on the following passages with the intention to soak your mind and emotions in the truth and allow the Holy Spirit to highlight specific parts that are pertinent to you.

Romans 10:10 (NASB):

"For with the heart a person believes, resulting in righteousness, and with the mouth he confesses, resulting in salvation."

Romans 5:1 (NASB):

"Therefore, having been justified by faith, we have peace with God through our Lord Jesus Christ."

Romans 1:17 (NASB):

"For in it the righteousness of God is revealed from faith to faith; as it is written, 'But the righteous man shall live by faith.'"

Romans 3:28 (NASB):

"For we maintain that a person is justified by faith apart from works of the Law."

Philippians 3:8–11 (NASB):

More than that, I count all things to be loss in view of the surpassing value of knowing Christ Jesus my Lord, for whom I have suffered the loss of all things, and count them mere rubbish so that I may gain Christ, and may be found in Him, not having a righteousness of my own derived from the Law, but that which is through faith in Christ, the righteousness which comes from God on the basis of faith, that I may know Him and the power of His resurrection and the fellowship of His sufferings, being conformed to His death; in order that I may attain to the resurrection from the dead.

Chapter 13

Dealing with Discouragement

"...and the soul of the people was much discouraged because of the way."

Numbers 21:4 (KJV)

Dealing with Discouragement

And they journeyed from Mount Hor by the way to the Red Sea, to compass the land of Edom: and the soul of the people was much discouraged because of the way. And the people spake against God, and against Moses, Wherefore have ye brought us up out of Egypt to die in the wilderness? For there is no bread, and there is no water; and our soul loatheth this light bread.

And Jehovah sent fiery serpents among the people, and they bit the people; and much people of Israel died. And the people came to Moses, and said, We have sinned, because we have spoken against Jehovah, and against thee; pray unto Jehovah, that He take away the serpents from us.

And Moses prayed for the people. And Jehovah said unto Moses, Make thee a fiery serpent, and set it upon a standard: and it shall come to pass, that every one that is bitten, when he looketh upon it, shall live. And Moses made a serpent of brass, and set it upon the standard: and it came to pass, that if a serpent had bitten any man, when he looked unto the serpent of brass, he lived.

Numbers 21:4–9 (KJV)

There is much that can be learned from this passage describing what happened to the Israelites as they journeyed with God to the promised land.

We will look at a couple of things here: First, the people became discouraged within their soul, and second, they grumbled against God and their leader. It is important to note that the Israelites sinned because they grumbled against God and their leader, not because they were discouraged. In our journey into our "promised land" and during times of delay, especially extended delay, we will often find discouragement arises within us. This, in itself, is not the sin that is being judged with the sending of fiery serpents. It is the grumbling that God responds to.

What does this mean for you when, in times of delay, your heart becomes discouraged? Well, the word for discouraged in Hebrew is *qatsar*, which also means to "grieve or mourn." It is at this place that God wants to meet us personally and intimately.

In Isaiah 61, we read that the Spirit of the Lord wants to "comfort all who mourn," and when Jesus spoke of the Holy Spirit in John 14, He used the word "comforter." So discouragement on the journey is not something the Lord wants us to suppress or see as sin, but He wants to be the One who comforts and ministers directly to our discouragement and grief when it arises. What I want to gently alert you to is that if we do not grieve, we cannot be comforted.

Allowing our hearts to be comforted is an important part of growing closer to the Lord, as well as letting go of what often hinders us from receiving the promises.

When we lose a loved one, grieving is a very important part of the process as we adapt to a life without that person. Often, the grieving process looks different for everyone, both on an emotional level but also regarding the timeline. No one would dare to condemn a person who was experiencing grief. We would encourage them to continue through their process with patience and care. However, when we ourselves experience grief and discouragement, we attempt to resist or fight it. The Holy Spirit does not only have the ability to comfort; He *is* comfort. So please do not resist, suppress, or fight the discouragement and grief that may be arising during this time of delay. Invite the Lord into it. The part we do want to resist is the temptation to grumble against God and those who He has placed over us in leadership and authority. Personally, this is where I have struggled over the years, not realizing that behind it was deep grief and the need for comfort. I allowed a suspicion against the Lord's intentions for me to arise, and when I entertained it, I would often have an inner dialogue of grumbling against God.

This is what the Lord wants us to resist because the consequences are extremely harmful. The wonderful thing about the Holy Spirit is He will show us where we have allowed the discouragement to turn into grumbling and self-pity.

With the people of God, the route they took to the promised land was what led to the discouragement.

In the visual below, you can see how instead of journeying directly to the promised land from Ezion Geber, they went up to the wilderness of Zin and then circled back down to Ezion Geber when Edom did not give them permission to cross their land, which would have felt like wasted time and energy.

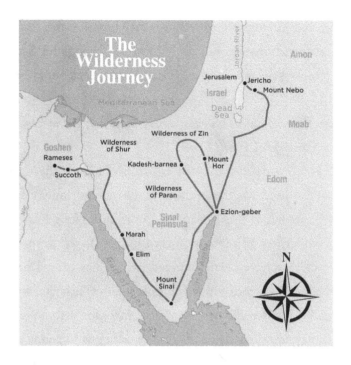

For the Lord, however, the main purpose of the journey through the wilderness was one of intimacy with Him. Removing the slave mindset and developing trust with Him would take time. Although I am sure the people of God wanted to go directly to Canaan, God's purpose was a higher one, and so too is it with us. The journey we are on with the Lord may look like it is taking an opposite turn from the one we are ultimately desiring, but He often does it for our protection. The delay of taking a longer journey to get to the promises has one main purpose in the eyes of the Lord, intimacy!

Delay, which so often feels like an unnecessary journey through the wilderness, has a precious purpose much higher than our soul and mind are able to comprehend. The Lord Himself desires our trust and longs for intimate connection with us. Throughout Scripture, the wilderness is the place where He does that. Check out Hosea 2:14 (NASB):

"Therefore, behold, I am going to persuade her, Bring her into the wilderness, and speak kindly to her."

The Hebrew word translated as "kindly" here is the word *leb*, which is also used for the mind, will, heart, and inner man (the soul). We see that in this passage, the Lord is drawing His beloved into the wilderness. His intention is to speak into the deepest parts of her soul that have been wounded, which has caused her grief and disconnection from Him. The Lord desires intimacy with His beloved, and He is willing to do what it takes for it to be restored. While it may seem like this passage is referring to someone else, we are the Lord's beloved. It is us that He is pursuing by drawing us into a place of intimacy with Him. Although at times, the delay may feel like a wilderness or the journey away from the promise, it is because the Lord wants to cultivate *true* intimacy with us.

When discouragement does come up, it sounds like, "God does not care," "God has forgotten me," "I have no value to God," etc., etc., and grumbling will be a result if we allow it. Over and over, I have ministered to children of God in this area, and the changing of perspective puts us in a position where we can allow our heart to be comforted and healed. It is incredibly powerful.

What is also powerful is that, in order to stop the judgment of the fiery serpents, Moses was instructed to put the very image of the fiery serpent up on a pole and have the people who were bitten look at it to receive their healing. There is much to be said about this picture, but I will only highlight that the serpent that Moses raised up on the pole was a foreshadowing of Christ being raised up on the cross. Jesus did not just take our sin upon Himself. He actually became sin. Think about it for a moment, as it seems absurd to liken Jesus to the serpent, but Jesus had to become sin for us, and when He did, He dealt with it once and for all on the cross. The Israelites were told to look at the serpent on the pole and they would be healed, just as we are to fix our eyes on Jesus, who became sin, and through Him, we are saved, healed, delivered! The Amplified Translation (AMPC) in Hebrews 12:2 says, "*Looking away [from all that will distract] to Jesus, Who is the Leader and the Source of our faith...*"

This speaks of repentance. If you have been struggling with grumbling, bring it before the Lord now. Look at the One who has taken away your sin and allow His Spirit to rise and deal with what is behind it: discouragement. He longs to comfort you. He longs for you to feel and experience His closeness. He is so close to you! The Lord cares very much about you! He is after your heart, and this time of delay is not a punishment but a pursuit of your heart as His beloved!

When we understand that the delay is not a punishment but a wooing of the Lord into greater intimacy, we can then shift our posture from defense to openness and vulnerability. In this place, the pain that arises in our heart in the form of discouragement and grief can be comforted. We can move toward Him rather than away. We can run into His arms instead of trying to shut down our intimacy with Him.

Take time now with the Lord in a time of reflection.

Reflection Questions

What spoke to you the most from this chapter?

_____

_____

_____

_____

_____

Why is it that discouragement can lead to grumbling?

_____

_____

_____

_____

_____

Can you see anywhere in your life where you are discouraged and have grumbled to yourself or to others?

_____

_____

_____

_____

_____

What would a lifestyle of allowing the Holy Spirit to comfort you look like?

_____

_____

_____

_____

_____

Spend some time journaling, asking the Lord to comfort you where you feel discouragement and grief.

_____

_____

_____

_____

_____

Strategies of War:
Returning to the Original Habitation

Chapter 14

Strengthen Yourself in the Lord

"But David strengthened himself in the Lord his God."

1 Samuel 30:6 (ESV)

Returning to the Original Habitation

In the chapter on facing the fire, I shared what the Lord revealed to me in Daniel 3: that it is completely possible to come out of this season without any evidence of having been in it. Foundational to this is a mindset or rather a *strategy* of warfare—to live as if you already have what you are waiting for. When the answers finally come and your prayers have been answered, your mind is already transformed, your heart expectant, and you are ready to *fully* receive.

History shows us that times of war and battle have a way of cultivating poverty mindsets as well as emotional scars that continue to torment a person even after the war is over and a new season of peace, provision, and abundance has begun. I have spoken to many war veterans and also to civilians who survived while family members went out to war. What I have come to find out through my conversations is that war has a way of impacting us, no matter how young we are when we go through it. Trauma and post-traumatic stress are serious issues that can leave us debilitated and unable to live a normal life, let alone the abundant life Jesus paid such a high price for.

I have noticed this happens to many believers experiencing delay, especially extended delay to answered prayers. The stress of the internal pressure can feel much like a battlefield, and the impact on the mind and emotions like a bombardment of enemy fire aimed to kill, steal, and destroy our faith. However, the Lord is showing us it is possible to come through this "enemy attack" almost unscathed and empowered for the new season of opportunities that are to come.

> The point of this book lies in knowing that the answer to coming out unscathed is not at the end of the battle but in what takes place within our soul during the waiting.

What looks like the presence of destruction is actually bringing perspective on the Father's love, His kingdom, His training to be an overcomer, and the power of the Holy Spirit to heal all wounds mentally, emotionally, and physically that have come from combat.

To get to this place of understanding, we have to also realize there is a strategy that we must use. For any challenge we are called to face, the Lord provides us with a blueprint on how to successfully overcome and experience victory. Here are some of the strategies and tools the Lord has shown me over the years that you can implement in your lifestyle.

Strengthen Yourself in the Lord before Inquiring of Him

King David knew warfare. He was skilled and one of the Bible's greatest warriors. David is known as a "man after God's own heart" (1 Samuel 13:14), and despite his own personal shortcomings, the way David responded to the challenges he faced gives us incredible insight and wisdom on how to deal with delay when the battle that comes looks impossible to win. First Samuel 30:1–8 (NASB) highlights this very well:

> *Then it happened when David and his men came to Ziklag on the third day, that the Amalekites had made a raid on*

the Negev and on Ziklag, and had overthrown Ziklag and burned it with fire; and they took captive the women and all who were in it, both small and great, without killing anyone, and carried them off and went their way. When David and his men came to the city, behold, it was burned with fire, and their wives and their sons and their daughters had been taken captive. Then David and the people who were with him lifted their voices and wept until there was no strength in them to weep.

Now David's two wives had been taken captive, Ahinoam the Jezreelitess and Abigail the widow of Nabal the Carmelite. Moreover David was greatly distressed because the people spoke of stoning him, for all the people were embittered, each one because of his sons and his daughters. But David strengthened himself in the Lord his God.

Then David said to Abiathar the priest, the son of Ahimelech, "Please bring me the ephod." So Abiathar brought the ephod to David. David inquired of the Lord, saying, "Shall I pursue this band? Shall I overtake them?" And He said to him, "Pursue, for you will surely overtake them, and you will surely rescue all."

When the situation seemed to be the opposite of what the Lord had prophesied and declared over David (which was He would be Israel's next king), the first thing David did was strengthen himself in the Lord before asking the Lord anything concerning his situation. Why is this significant? Well, if you are anything like me, you may tend to run boldly before the throne of grace and beg the Lord to show up for you, pushing for answers that are desperately needed. This was not David's pattern. He chose to strengthen himself first before approaching the Lord.

Our need for understanding can often affect our trust in the Lord. Yet, one of the most famous scriptures, Proverbs 3:5–6 (ESV), says just the opposite, *"Trust in the Lord your God with all your heart, and do not lean on your own understanding, in all your ways acknowledge Him and He will make your path straight."*

To put it another way:

> When we push first for understanding, it is simply praying from the problem.

Rather than praying from the place of our solution and victory in the throne room of God, we end up devaluing the position we have as a child of God.

We become beggars, looking for answers like we are victims of our circumstances. Think about this for a moment. How many of your prayers are fueled by anxiety? Anxiety naturally accompanies us when we decide to pray from the problem rather than from the place where we are strengthened in the Lord, a place fueled with peace, purpose, power, and gratefulness.

Praying from the problem is about us; praying from a place of being strengthened in God is about Him.

Strengthening yourself in the Lord positions you to hear from God and respond from a place of freedom and authority. The ways to strengthen yourself in the Lord are endless. Worship, declaration of the Word, taking communion, and praying in the Spirit are all examples of how you can do this. Whatever you are led to do, the key is to focus on Him, His righteousness in you, and His mighty work around you, in you, to you, and through you.

The focus is on truth, not facts. This will help you to remember what He has said and done for you. Instead of your emotions and thoughts being focused on the problem, you are now able to *fully* focus on the solution, your heavenly Father! Jude 1:20 (NIV) calls it, *"...building yourselves up in your most Holy faith..."*

My greatest desire is that as you read this book, you will become as convinced as I am that the Father longs to reveal the power of Jesus' resurrection available to you. Answers will come; breakthrough is yours, but the journey to get there can be made so much sweeter with this strategy of strengthening yourself in Him before you seek information from Him about your problem.

Reflection Questions

How have you noticed yourself coming before the Lord in times of inner crisis? Are you focused on your situation and begging Him for intervention?

_____

_____

_____

_____

_____

In what ways can you cultivate a pattern where you automatically go to strengthen yourself in the Lord before you ask Him for information about your situation?

_____

_____

_____

_____

_____

How can you incorporate some of the teachings from this chapter into your response mechanism?

_____

_____

_____

_____

_____

Chapter 15

Compassion Destroys the Yoke of Shame

"When He went ashore, He saw a large crowd, and felt [profound] compassion for them and healed their sick."

Matthew 14:14 (AMP)

Compassion Is Comfort

In the first part of this book, I shared how shame and the cycle that develops from it can keep us from receiving the very thing we actually need: the compassion of the Lord. Compassion is comfort, and it has taken me a while to allow my heart to be vulnerable before the Lord to truly receive His compassion. My tendency, and what I now realize is the same for many of us, is that we want answers and feel shame in the midst of the uncertainty. Therefore, we never truly allow our heart to be comforted and experience the healing compassion provides.

Receiving compassion is like a child who has fallen and hurt himself on the playground and comes running to his mommy. The first thing she does is pick him up, and she comforts him, letting him know she is there. While he is screaming inconsolably, she lovingly tells him everything is okay. Holding him close, she rocks him until he is calm again and peace is restored. This is a natural inner response from the parent, and only after the child has calmed down does she tend to the wound on her child's knee.

Often, a child will not even need a Band-Aid once he or she has been comforted by his or her parent. It is also not uncommon for that same child to soon be back playing as if nothing has happened. Getting the child "calm" through compassion is the first thing the mother does, and it is also what our heavenly Father wants to do for us. However, many of us do not know we need comfort, let alone how to receive it. We want answers and the problem fixed immediately.

Then, and only then, will everything be okay. But will it be? When we encounter a great challenge like waiting on God to fulfill a long-awaited promise, that promise does not have to be fulfilled before we feel "safe" again. It is like the child with his mother. At first, it may seem we may need a Band-Aid for the pain when, in reality, what we really need is comfort, which will calm our nervous system and reset everything back into balance.

For the longest time, it has been my tendency to run to the Lord for that Band-Aid when I am in pain. I convinced myself that if He could just give me a quick solution, then I would be fine. The thing is, I never end up feeling fine. Unable to receive the comfort that I truly need, the pressure of my current situation feels like a subtle blanket on me, making life seem dull and dreary. Well, at least until I manage to pull myself out of it and carry on. This is what many of us do. We go to get solutions and answers because of the stress and pain of delay, and instead of getting the comfort we need, we pull ourselves together and carry on. If you are like me, then this is your pattern in response to pain. You have probably become very good at keeping yourself together despite what is going on in your life. This is actually a learned behavior, picked up in the environment and culture we have grown up in.

The issue with compassion is that it takes time. It sits with us in our moment of pain to calm us, to bring our heart and nervous system back to equilibrium, but this is not always quick. Most cultures are fast-paced and have little time for just being present in the pain, in the need. What I have noticed from the many, many hundreds of hours of ministering to others is that almost every person has transferred this fast-paced behavior to their walk with God.

What we have to understand is that receiving compassion is a key part to remaining in a place of peace during times of waiting and hard times in general.

Compassion Is Who Jesus Was and Is Today

Compassion is used many times to describe Jesus, and it was always connected to when He performed a healing or a miracle. Let us look at a few examples. Matthew 20:34 (NASB), in the healing of two blind men, says, *"Moved with compassion, Jesus touched their eyes; and immediately they regained their sight and followed Him."* In Luke 7:13–15 (NASB), when Jesus met a widow whose son had died, *"... He felt compassion for her, and said to her, 'Do not weep.' And He came up and touched the coffin; and the bearers came to a halt. And He said, 'Young man, I say to you, arise!' ...the dead man sat up and began to speak."* Then, in Matthew 14:14 (NASB), *"when He came ashore, He saw a large crowd, and felt compassion for them and healed their sick."*

Unfortunately, when discussing these passages, most pastors skip past the compassion piece and go straight to the miracles Jesus performed. As we see, in order for healing and miracles to be demonstrated, compassion must also be present. Something worth mentioning is when we look at the Greek meaning for compassion, we get the word *splagchnizomai*, which literally means "to be moved in the inward parts." It was this deep reaction from within that moved Jesus to action.

Compassion for You

I want to clarify that compassion is not pity or simply sympathy. Compassion is the deep emotive affection for another person. When we read about Jesus being moved with compassion, it was for a person or a group of people. Jesus is also moved with compassion for you. It is you He is moved by. Yes, He cares about what is happening to you and the impact this delay, lack, and the things you have experienced have had on you, but, first and foremost, He is moved with compassion for you! Why is this important for you to know? Because you are what Jesus is focused on. Like the example with the mother and her child in the park, she is focused on the emotional well-being of her child, not the injury, which can be easily cleaned up. When you are stuck in the shame cycle, your primary focus is on the solutions to your problem. However, when it comes to Jesus, His focus is on you receiving His compassion.

As demonstrated in the previous passages, Jesus was moved to respond toward those He saw hurting, hungry, or oppressed with deep affection, which then led to their healing as well as their spiritual, emotional, and mental freedom. Jesus is the same today as He was back then. He has not changed His ways. Even as you read this, He is moved with compassion for you right now. I want you to do me this favor: set aside your questions and your need for solutions because, in the next section, we are going to get to the root of it all.

Compassion Is the Antidote for Shame

The fascinating thing about receiving compassion or what feels to me like the Lord sitting there and comforting me is that it really does shift the wiring and chemical responses in the brain. Instead of the thoughts that once created stress, a powerful trigger for me, there is a calm response. The need for answers regarding my situation is no longer an issue, and the more I have practiced receiving compassion, the more my response has changed, and I see things differently. My eyes have been opened to who I really am; receiving becomes easier, and this is not a phenomenon only achievable by me. You, too, can experience this once you allow yourself to receive the compassion of our Lord, Jesus.

God's Response in the Garden Was Compassion

Many people look at what happened in the garden of Eden from the perspective of God being angry with Adam and Eve, but is this really the full picture? His compassion and His longing to be in relationship with them were there in plain sight. When God asked, "Adam, where are you?" He knew where Adam was. How could He not? He is God. The question was not to shame Adam but to draw him out, draw him close, and draw him back into a relationship with His Father.

This same God desires to give you compassion, but if you feel you are not enough, you cannot receive it because you are hidden behind the big emotions.

Another Comforter

In two of my favorite chapters, John 14 and 16, Jesus talks about the Father sending the Holy Spirit to us and refers to Him as the Comforter. Jesus, who is compassionate Himself, is saying, "I will send another comforter." This is Jesus' response to humanity because He knows we need His comfort and compassion. Being comforted is more important than we think. Matthew 5, also known as the "beatitudes" chapter, describes Jesus' attitude toward those who need to be comforted, *"Blessed are those who mourn, for they shall be comforted"* (Matthew 5:4, NKJV).

He calls them *blessed*.

You see, it is a blessing for us to need comforting because it allows us to encounter the compassion of the Father, which, ultimately, is the tender expression of His love and care toward us through Jesus and the impartation of the Holy Spirit. I encourage you today to allow yourself to grieve. Whether it is directly connected to what you are waiting for or the past, it does not matter. The Comforter wants to meet you in this place of grief and bring you back to wholeness.

Ask yourself if what you are feeling is actually disconnection, shame, or abandonment. In this next section, you will find tools that I learned from Laura Duncan, a true minister of compassion, that will help you process your emotions when you feel triggered.

Here are a few practical ways to practice receiving compassion:

1) Picture yourself in a time of need, maybe now or younger. Ask the Holy Spirit to help you do this.

Not everyone finds it easy to visualize Jesus. So picture someone you felt safe and loved by. It could be a grandparent, an aunt, a dear family friend, etc. Visualize them just coming to you in that moment of need. Remember, like the child at the playground, you do not need your wound fixed yet; you need comfort.

Sit with your feelings. Identify and name what you are feeling. At first, it may be a hard emotion like anger, betrayal, resentment, hatred, or fear, but keep asking yourself, "What am I really feeling?" Identify the feelings and write them here.

Hard emotions:

_____

_____

_____

_____

Soft emotions:

_____

_____

_____

_____

Read through the list below. Pick the words that connect with your heart. What is compassion for one person may not be compassion for another. Read the phrases that stand out to you. Slowly say them to yourself. Let your heart receive the nurture, comfort, and healing that these words bring.

Here are some compassion words that are soothing:

I see you trying so hard. I am proud of you.

I am sorry you feel sad.

I am sorry you feel alone. I am sorry you feel scared.

I can tell you care so much. Take all the time you need. You are going to be okay.

I will sit with you until you feel safe. I accept you.

I value you.

I am sorry you feel trapped. I think you are brave.

I don't want to get rid of you. I don't see you as broken.

I see you.

I enjoy you.

2) This second exercise is one you can learn to do anytime and anywhere when you are feeling triggered. a) Pause the trigger (person, circumstance, or thought) for a moment. What is the trigger?

_____

_____

_____

_____

b) What do you feel? Keep asking yourself this question until you get past the hard emotions (*angry, out-of-control, frustrated, etc.*). Connect to tender emotions (*sad, scared, lonely, etc.*).

Hard emotions:

_____

_____

_____

_____

Soft emotions:

_____

_____

_____

_____

3) Based on your answer to how you are feeling, ask yourself what you need. Example: *If I feel sad, I need to feel comforted and loved.*

I need:

_____

_____

_____

_____

4) Show yourself compassion. Treat yourself the way that you would treat your child, spouse, or someone close to you. Show yourself care, consideration, and tenderness.

Compassionate feelings and words:

_____

_____

_____

_____

5) Unpause the trigger and now look at it through the eyes of being self-aware of your feelings. From your list, choose what you need and show yourself compassion.

How does the trigger feel now?

_____

_____

_____

_____

The more times you do this process, the better you will become. So give yourself grace to not always get it right. If you are connected to your heart, you will have peace even if your circumstances do not change right away.

_____

_____

_____

_____

Chapter 16

Developing Comparison Resilience

"Don't compare your journey with someone else's.

Your journey is your journey, not a competition."

—Anonymous

Developing Comparison Resilience

Comparison and its effects on our soul are toxic.

Every day we are bombarded with physical realities we see and hear that cause us to compare and judge ourselves constantly. The billboards in the towns and cities we live in, the supermarkets where we shop, and the TV and phones we look at every day are all designed to make sure we compare what we have, how we look, and how much money is in our bank account, all to create a need to desire what is being sold to us. This need rises often out of a sense of lack, and because it happens daily, that pattern can become very familiar to us. At the root of comparison is the belief that someone else's gain is our loss, which then translates into having an atmosphere of lack within the soul.

Even as believers, we are not immune to comparison. Sadly, envy, strife, jealousy, and contention become a common part of church life when comparison is not dealt with.

While the hard reality is we cannot fully escape the tactics that breed comparison, there is still hope for us to lessen the effects on us. Once we understand what is going on and why, we can come to a place where we learn to resist any negative forms of comparison.

The beautiful advantage we have as believers is having the Holy Spirit work within us. He lovingly reveals the areas where we struggle with comparison and helps us to renew our minds.

You see, the kingdom of God does not function on the same principles as the world does.

First, someone else's gain is not our lack in the kingdom. There is always enough for everyone.

Each of us is running our own race. Not against each other but according to what the Lord has called, gifted, and chosen us to do. The writer of Hebrews says in 12:1–2 (NIV), *"...let us throw off everything that hinders and the sin that so easily entangles. And let us run with perseverance the race marked out for us, fixing our eyes on Jesus, the pioneer and perfecter of faith."*

Therefore, to compare ourselves to one another serves no value for us because we are the only ones in our race. The course that has been set was marked out for us alone! God knows the plans He has for us, and they are to prosper us (Jeremiah 29:11). His plans are intended to give us hope and a future. So, you see, beloved, God's intentions toward you are *always* good.

I am going to share a picture with you, and then I want you to close your eyes and reflect on it.

Picture yourself in a race. There is a road in front of you and stunning scenery all around. There are valleys and hills, and you are pacing yourself as you run this race. There is also heavenly encouragement in the atmosphere, surrounding you and cheering you forward. You see other runners, and they cross your path. Some even run alongside you for a while, but you also see that they have a path of their own, much different from yours.

Some runners look like they are running straight up the mountain that is just ahead, but then their path disappears into a crevasse, and you cannot see what they are going through. Others seem to be on a smoother and easier path. However, you, at no point, can see every aspect of each runner's path, and this is okay. Every path, no matter how different, leads to the top of the same mountain, and everything that you or the other runners may need is on each specific path.

Recognizing that no path is better or worse but rather designed specifically for each runner, you all spur each other on as you pass by one another. Feel how the pressure to perform is released from you when competition is taken out of the equation, and suddenly, the scenery, the exhilaration of the journey, comes more into view. Now take this visual and reflect on it more, allowing the Holy Spirit to highlight your path in a pictorial way during your delay.

Second, I want you to understand that your blessings are not earned but a gift of grace. So you need not compare yourself. In the kingdom of God, He meets all your needs according to His glorious riches in Christ Jesus: *"But my God shall supply all your need according to His riches in glory by Christ Jesus"* (Philippians 4:19, KJV).

Here it is written that He meets *the* need rather than needs. The Greek word used is *chreia,* which literally means "need or necessity." Ultimately, we have only one need in the kingdom of God, and that is Jesus. He is the Tree of Life, the one who, by His grace, gives us all things. Hence the reason He can say, *"That is why I tell you not to worry about everyday life..."* (Matthew 6:25, NLT). We can fix our eyes on Him if we know that our need is Him and that, in Him, all things pertaining to life are met. This puts us in a receiving mode rather than a comparison and striving mode to earn what has already been given to us freely.

How to Become Resilient

The temptation to compare is high, and I encourage you to train yourself to become resistant to it. This is something the Holy Spirit taught me, and it needs to develop much like a muscle in exercise. Like all things, awareness is the first of the criteria to change.

In fact, when it comes to health and fitness, awareness is 90 percent of change. This is great because as you read this and you sense this activity in your heart, that awareness in itself is the greatest step toward your transformation in this area.

Once you know that comparison is toxic, pointless, and damaging to your relationship with God, yourself, and others, you can take a stand and resist the enemy.

> The key to resisting is refusing to entertain the negative thought that wants your attention.

Whether negative or positive, thoughts are seeds that get planted in the soil of our hearts and produce a harvest. In this case, since the thought is negative, what sprouts up is comparison, shame, condemnation, and separation from God. Learning how to use the sword of the Word of God and the shield of faith against the implantation of negative thoughts in our hearts will help us to maintain our peace in the face of great difficulty and challenge. This is us using our God-given authority to govern the land of our soul and keep it from being defiled. As we begin to use our authority and consciously take every negative thought captive, what we will find is the powerful emotions that stem from it will start to diminish. In some areas, it can take a little longer to see the change, but once we have experienced the peace that comes with submitting our thoughts to Christ, we have already started a new pattern.

Before we take this further, I want to impart to you how committed, loving, and gentle the Lord is with us in this area and how He helps to change the negative narrative we are living from by releasing His truth over us. What is an area for you where the narrative needs to change? Bring it to the forefront and celebrate the awareness that it is possible for it to actually change. Next, bring it into context with comparison and allow the Holy Spirit to highlight where in your life you are entertaining this thought. Take a step back, almost as if you are observing your own thought process. Listen to what your emotions are saying. If comparison is involved, you will usually hear negativity about yourself, God, and others.

Sometimes it comes in the form of impressions and strong emotions. Do not push them down, but take them before the Lord and ask Him for *His* narrative instead—what He sees, what He thinks. Allow the Word of God to rise up in you for this specific situation.

As you do this, you are taking your thoughts captive to Christ. This is where resisting comes in. The truth narrative the Lord has for you is what you can then entertain and allow to take root. At first, it can feel like discipline and a bit regimented, but the peace, joy, and sense of freedom you will receive, in the long run, are incredible.

It also helps to contemplate on the areas in your life where you have already learned to resist destructive thoughts and use those victories as a form of encouragement for yourself. For example, once I knew the Lord had set me apart for marriage, sexual purity became very important to me. I had to learn how to resist sexual temptation. I had to make sure I did not look at men the wrong way, which also meant no double takes when I saw a good-looking man or watching sexual scenes on TV, etc. Before long, a pattern of resisting developed, and I became resilient in this area. It would be a flat-out lie for me to tell you that sexual thoughts do not come up from time to time. After all, I am human. The difference is I know that entertaining these thoughts only leads down a destructive path, so I choose to close the door by giving them no room to grow. This is how I claim victory, and you can as well.

God is committed to you being free of comparison, and one of the ways you will know you are getting free is the joy you experience within. You will find yourself less triggered by your circumstance and able to rejoice with those who have attained their promise without the inner dialogue of comparison taking place. It may seem like getting to this level of freedom is impossible, but all it takes is one thought at a time to be brought under the authority of Jesus Christ. This is not an easy task to do. However, it is possible. The Holy Spirit is with you, and He is cheering you on.

You can, and you will overcome this.

Reflection Questions

How does the culture you live in cultivate a habit of comparison?

_____

_____

_____

_____

_____

In what areas have you struggled with comparison as you have waited? Why is it so toxic for the soul? Can you see how it affects your life?

_____

_____

_____

_____

_____

What does your race look like, and how does looking at the big picture of life help you resist comparison?

_____

_____

_____

_____

_____

What does comparison reveal about your deepest desires?

_____

_____

_____

_____

_____

In what area in your life have you learned to resist the temptation to entertain destructive thoughts?

_____

_____

_____

_____

_____

Chapter 17

Sow into What You Are Waiting For

"For with the measure you use, it will be measured to you."

Luke 6:38 (NIV)

Sow into What You Are Waiting For

When Jesus spoke on the kingdom, He shared this:

"Give, and it will be given to you. A good measure, pressed down, shaken together and running over, will be poured into your lap. For with the measure you use, it will be measured to you" (Luke 6:38, NIV).

I may not be married yet, but I can sow into and bless every marriage that I come into contact with. I may not have children yet, but I sow life into all the children I meet, especially my nieces and nephews, who I know I can have a huge impact on. We do not earn our salvation or even have to earn the gifts and promises of God, but faith without works is dead. The Holy Spirit stirs us to act on what we are believing, and because I am believing for a kingdom marriage and children, during this time of waiting, I have intentionally sown into that which I wish to receive.

In the same respect, as God has heightened my desire to see cities and nations transformed, I have sown into the very movement of movements that is making this a reality on earth, Transform Our World.

It has all been quite fascinating if you ask me. What I have noticed is that not only does this intentional action of sowing take our eyes off ourselves, which is important, but it simultaneously cultivates a lifestyle of giving. It helps us laugh in the face of lack and builds us up emotionally and mentally as we realize how rich we are in the kingdom and just how much life and love are available to us today. Sowing the seeds of faith into the area where we want to reap a harvest is a powerful concept and one not to be taken lightly. Let's be clear: this is not about earning anything but believing through faith action that we will receive what we have been promised by our heavenly Father.

Reflection Questions

Where could you be sowing, giving, and blessing right now? The amount is not the focus. It is about your heart's intention.

_____

_____

_____

_____

_____

Let the Holy Spirit make this personal for you. What resources do you have? Time? Money?

_____

_____

_____

_____

_____

Chapter 18

Developing a Grateful Heart

"Let joy be your continual feast. Make your life a prayer. And in the midst of everything be always giving thanks, for this is God's perfect plan for you in Christ Jesus."

1 Thessalonians 5:16–18 (TPT)

Developing a Grateful Heart

"Be careful for nothing; but in every thing by prayer and supplication with thanksgiving let your requests be made known unto God. And the peace of God, which passeth all understanding, shall keep your hearts and minds through Christ Jesus" (Philippians 4:6–7, KJV).

Developing a grateful heart has much to do with strengthening yourself in the Lord. Yet, it deserves a section of its own because of the sheer power it has to impact our daily lives. Interestingly, I have noticed this is one of the hardest things to do when we are in pain or feeling any sense of lack. Pain has a way of preventing us from seeing the truth of our reality, which is we have more than we need to prosper in this current season.

Gratefulness, however, keeps us in the present moment and aware of what we do have. The long-term impact of intentionally practicing this is incredible. Gratefulness increases joy, which is like "good medicine" for the heart (Proverbs 17:22, ESV).

In the last ten years, there have been many scientific studies done on the impact of gratefulness on our health and immunology. What they have concluded is there is a direct correlation between gratefulness and overall good mental and physical health. Many of these studies have been done using gratitude journals as well as other forms to practice gratitude. All seem to show that gratitude causes the brain to release dopamine and serotonin. These are the two crucial neurotransmitters responsible for the emotions that make us feel good. They enhance our mood immediately, making us feel happy, which has a downstream effect of improving our physical health by reducing stress and inflammation and improving sleep. Besides helping people sleep better, gratitude leads people to engage in other behaviors that help keep them healthy, like eating well and not smoking.

By consciously practicing gratitude, we can help these neural pathways strengthen themselves and, ultimately, create a permanent grateful nature within ourselves, positively impacting our physical and psychological well-being for years to come.

How to Develop Gratefulness

First, make it an intentional discipline for the next forty days. Every morning, when you wake up, thank God for three things. Then, before you go to sleep, thank Him for three things you were grateful for that happened on that day. For the first couple of days, the things you find yourself grateful for may be exactly the same, and that is okay. The more you intentionally practice gratefulness, you will find yourself thanking God for things as you shower, as you get ready, and throughout the rest of your day.

Second, start a gratitude journal and write in it daily. Write down the three things that you are grateful for. Depending on where you are emotionally, it can sometimes be challenging to think of three things to be grateful for. If this is you, then start with one thing.

As you do this activity, pay attention to what you are feeling and how it is affecting you. Make sure to note any changes in your stress levels, emotions, or physical body movement.

You can then take it a stage further. Write down the three things you are grateful for and then write down the response you hear from the Lord. This will further develop intimacy and His response to your heart more and more.

Chapter 19

Perseverance

Gratefulness increases joy. And "a joyful heart is good medicine..."

Proverbs 17:22 (ISV)

Perseverance

So here we have one of the most powerful strategies for coming through the fire of delay, and that is: don't give up. It does not matter whether you have a history of giving up easily or not. At the point of your salvation, your spirit was made alive with an innate ability to persevere and overcome. Now that you are at this point in the book, I want to encourage you to start making a conscious decision to not give up, to not let go of God's promises, dreams, and desires for you.

As you process through those powerful emotions we discussed earlier and learn to control and govern your soul, you will find it easier to focus on the One who never lies.

Read Romans 5:3–5 (TPT) with me:

> But that's not all! Even in times of trouble we have a joyful confidence, knowing that our pressures will develop in us patient endurance. And patient endurance will refine our character, and proven character leads us back to hope. And this hope is not a disappointing fantasy, because we can now experience the endless love of God cascading into our hearts through the Holy Spirit who lives in us!

Again, I want to emphasize that the soul is not bad. But what we do see is that our soul will accept facts as evidence even when the facts are contrary to the truth of God's Word. So ministering to your soul is like receiving the justice Jesus spoke of in the parable of the unjust judge. In the gospel of Luke, there is a fascinating parable in chapter 18 that Jesus shares. This is where God gave me the revelation to persevere when all the facts looked opposite to the truth of His Word over my life.

The parable reflects the battle we face within our souls when fear is impacting our hearts to the point where we struggle to believe what we know is ours by faith.

Then Jesus told His disciples a parable to show them that they should always pray and not give up. He said: "In a certain town there was a judge who neither feared God nor cared what people thought. And there was a widow in that town who kept coming to him with the plea, 'Grant me justice against my adversary.' For some time he refused. But finally, he said to himself, 'Even though I don't fear God or care what people think, yet because this widow keeps bothering me, I will see that she gets justice, so that she won't eventually come and attack me!'" And the Lord said, "Listen to what the unjust judge says. And will not God bring about justice for His chosen ones, who cry out to Him day and night? Will He keep putting them off?

I tell you, He will see that they get justice, and quickly. However, when the Son of Man comes, will He find faith on the earth?"

Luke 18:1–8 (NIV)

The last sentence in this passage gives away the context of what Jesus is wanting to get across. When the Son of Man comes, will He find faith on earth? In other words, will Jesus find belief?

It was a few years back when I heard a message on the unjust judge being the soul of man and the persistent widow being our spirit's persistence to see God's truth reign. The usual representation of this parable with God as the unjust judge and our need to persistently press through to Him always made me feel uneasy, as it seemed out of character for Jesus to dishonor the character of His Father by relating Him to the unjust judge.

As you read the New Testament and start to understand the covenant we have in Christ Jesus, you will see over and over how important faith is when it comes to receiving all that God has prepared for us and promised us through the precious sacrifice of His Son. Believing is the key focus in this covenant:

"All things are possible for one who believes" (Mark 9:23, ESV).

"Without Faith it is impossible to please Him" (Hebrews 11:6, KJV).

"Did I not say if you believe, you will see the Glory of God?" (John 11:40, NASB).

> The soul, like the unjust judge, will accept facts as evidence even when they are contrary to the truth of God's Word.

Ed Silvoso would call these strongholds in the mind, which we accept as unchangeable, something we know is contrary to the Word of God. In order for us to be transformed, our minds need to be renewed. Remember there is nothing wrong with your soul.

However, your mind does need renewing in the truth. Renewing your mind will cause you to be transformed and will give you access to all the blessings in the heavenly realms with Christ.

When we find ourselves facing a physical reality that is different from the promise of God, we can get confused about the character of God and His heart toward us, which then leads to disqualifying ourselves through unbelief. Getting us to question the character of God and His heart toward us has been the plan of the evil one from the very beginning. The first question he asked Eve was, *"Did God really say...?"* (Genesis 3:1, NIV). As a result, she then became suspicious of the One who was actually invested in her success! Ed Silvoso also talks about applying the Word of God as a treatment against the strongholds the enemy has set up in our minds. This strategy should be the tool that we use when learning to govern our soul by taking every thought captive.

As I have mentioned before, delay is like the fire burning under the pot of raw gold, bringing all the dross to the surface so it can be removed and the gold purified. Areas of unbelief, suspicion against God, and strongholds in our minds will have no choice but to come to the surface and be dealt with. The fire is meant to reveal that which can only be seen and experienced after being tested by it. Be encouraged. There is beauty and freedom on a level you have never experienced on the other side of this. Do not run or try to hide but stand in full confidence, knowing that facing this fire of delay will bring about a greater reward for you on earth and in heaven.

By the time you get to this part of the book, my hope is you will know you are not waiting in vain. Just as a pregnancy has many stages, so does the character God is developing in you. The framework of your faith is being built, and you are learning to trust Him more as you develop a greater intimacy with His nature. Never forget, with God, there is a purpose for everything, and when it comes to His children, it is always to draw them closer to Him.

Activation:

Find a comfortable place with the Lord and your journal. Ask Him to show you any area in your soul where you are accepting a lie over the truth.

_____

_____

_____

_____

_____

_____

Now ask the Lord to show you the truth. This may come in the form of a verse, a visual picture, or a phrase that aligns with the Word. Write it down.

_____

_____

_____

_____

_____

Like the widow, this is where you allow the persistence to come in. Spend time meditating on the truth that He has given you. You may feel a shift immediately, but, for many, it may take some time, hence the power of this parable.

_____

_____

_____

_____

_____

Final Exhortation

"We have this certain hope like a strong, unbreakable anchor holding our souls to God Himself."

Hebrews 6:19 (TPT)

Your soul needs hope. It anchors you to God Himself so you can weather the storms and waves that would knock you into the rocks like a boat.

Because your soul has been created for a spiritual habitation, this anchor serves you to remain in Him. Yes, this hope in God's unchanging nature is the *one* thing we *all* have that will bring us into the promises we are waiting for.

"May the God of hope fill you with all joy and peace as you trust in Him, so that you may overflow with hope by the power of the Holy Spirit" (Romans 15:13, NIV).

I write this closing exhortation as a single woman, but this anchor of hope is firmly embedded within me to the heart of God, so much so that what once created despair in me now serves me and has drawn me to such a place of assurance that I can now impart this hope in love and in power to everyone I meet. I tell you, today, God will not fail you!

My prayer for you is that every delay that you face from this moment on serves you rather than masters you. May the fire of delay bring you, like Shadrach, Meshach, and Abednego, into a place of security in who He is. May this hope anchor you in Him and make you unshakeable.

Rest assured, the promises *will be* fulfilled, and this is what your heavenly Father has to say to you, *"Have no doubt, I promise to bless you over and over..."* (Hebrews 6:14, TPT)

So wait patiently in faith, and you will succeed in seeing the promises fulfilled. Patience is His fruit. Your focus is not on gritting your teeth and waiting it out. It is on Him, and He is drawing you deeper and deeper into the revelation of who He is and, simultaneously, who you are. I have full confidence that you will see the goodness of God in the land of the living.

Heavenly Father, bless my sisters and brothers as the truth of Your love and goodness brings them through this fire of delay and into unimaginable realms of Your peace and goodness. May the eyes of their heart be enlightened to the hope that You have called them for the riches of their glorious inheritance as saints and the incomparable great power available toward them because they believe in You.

Father, may their souls experience more and more of the atmosphere of Your love and kingdom where all things are possible. May they be empowered to see through their current circumstance and into the kingdom realm, beyond the realities of facts, and live by faith and no longer just by sight.

Thank You that it is Your good pleasure to give them the kingdom, where grace abounds to them by faith and where timing is seen from a higher place. May they enjoy the riches of gold that is produced in the fire of delay and the promotion that comes with it. May they know how powerful they are to minister to their soul, to exhort and strengthen themselves in You, Lord, and enter Your rest, ceasing from their own striving.

You commend them for looking to Your nature as the foundation of their confidence, and You will fulfill what You have promised to each of them as Your beloved sons and daughters.

Bless them, Lord, fill them, Lord, guide them, and may Your delight in them manifest the desires of their heart.

In the name of Jesus Christ, amen.